CW01066466

THE POEMS

('CANTI')

OF

LEOPARDI

Done into English

BY

J. M. MORRISON, M.A.

GAY AND BIRD

22 BEDFORD STREET, STRAND

LONDON

1900

TRANSLATOR'S PREFACE.

GIACOMO LEOPARDI was born on June 29, 1798, at Recanati, a small country town in the March of Ancona. He was of noble descent on both father and mother's side, but the family was in somewhat straitened circumstances. His father, Count Leopardi, lived retired from the world, a pedant of narrow views, but of considerable erudition; a bigot who held ultramontane and mediæval notions as to the prerogatives and position of the clergy and the Church, whose almost servilely devoted son he was; a father who utterly failed, if indeed he ever tried, to understand his gifted son, or win his sympathy and affection. He destined Giacomo for the Church, and could never forgive him for his refusal to devote his life to her service.

The young Leopardi was sickly as a boy even, and his over-studious habits from his earliest years utterly undermined a constitution which would never have been robust. He spent his boyhood's days unchecked in his father's well-stocked library, omnivorously devouring and assimilating all that came to his hands, till at the age of sixteen already he had become a self-taught prodigy of learning. He had read through all the ancient classics, and mastered several European modern languages and Hebrew besides. At the same age, too, he had imposed on the ripest Italian scholars with two Anacreontic odes which he composed, and which were received as genuine ancient classics, and he had also written, besides other works giving evidence of precocious intellectual powers, a commentary on Porphyry's

Life of Plotinus. At eighteen he wrote the *Appressamento alla Morte*, a panegyric on the universal might and sway of Death.

For years Leopardi had chafed under the almost petty tyranny of his father and the restraint of his ungenial surroundings, and he sighed for Rome which seemed to his restless youthful dreams the only spot where his ambitions could find their fulfilment, and where he could devote to the service of his poor distracted Italy that intense patriotic fervour which burned within him, and which is so finely expressed in his first four *canti* (*To Italy*, etc.). It was not till 1822, however, that he could obtain his father's grudging consent to depart ; but, alas ! after a year's stay in the Eternal City, he returned disillusioned and broken-spirited to Recanati. During that interval he had made acquaintance with the German historian Niebuhr, then Papal Ambassador of Prussia at Rome. In 1825 Leopardi left Recanati a second time for Bologna and Milan, having been engaged by a publishing house of the latter city to edit Cicero and Plutarch for them. He also resided for some time in Florence before returning once more to his ancestral home, bowed down with disappointment and ill-health and threatened blindness. A rude awakening in Florence from a dream of love, whose object is referred to with such mingled despite and tenderness in *Aspasia* (page 113), proved the final shattering of whatever illusions and dreams he had left, and a death-blow to his last hopes. His ardent soul, imprisoned in a sickly, unattractive frame, craved and thirsted for love. He had to own, after bitter experience, that a woman's love was not for him. Can we wonder that with his supersensitive nature this conviction brought, if not humiliation, at least the depths of despondency? In 1832 he was again in Florence, where he met Ranieri, in whose intimacy he spent the last years of his life, and who was afterwards to act the part and gain the questionable dis-

tinction of another Trelawney to another equally ill-starred
Byron. Leopardi died at his friend's house in Naples rather
suddenly on June 15, 1837, a few days before the completion
of his thirty-ninth year.

Besides the precocious works mentioned and the *canti*
here translated, we have from Leopardi a considerable
amount of youthful poems and translations from the classics,
notably his long *Continuation of the Battle of Frogs and
Mice*. His fame rests, next to his *canti*, on his prose
Operette Morali, a series of dialogues on philosophy. These
are characterized throughout by the same pessimistic view
of life and human destiny as runs through his *canti*—the
conviction that all is vanity, that life is an empty thing and
death desirable ; that man's best efforts are vain, and human
nature as a whole addicted to and content with cringing and
sloth and vileness. He is the only true man who has eman-
cipated himself from the vulgar illusions of pleasures and the
things of sense, and has lifted himself up to the calm, clear
height where intellect reigns supreme and sole. But Leopardi's is never a whining, puling despair ; we are never
offended by it ; we feel that his was a lovable nature, as
indeed his best friends have told us. Whilst we pity his sad,
unhappy fate, we feel sure that under happier auspices and
with better health and more congenial environment, his
genius would have postulated a saner and less one-sided
view of life, and that though it could not have embraced a
more perfect expression and classic form, it would have taken
a more expansive range.

With regard to the present translation, if it is any justi-
fication for one's temerity in attempting what one of our
greatest living authorities and critics has pronounced to be
a task never likely to be accomplished adequately in our
language, may I say that several able renderings of the
canti have appeared in German, whilst they have been practi-
cally ignored with us? It seemed to me strange that England

should be left behind in an honest attempt at least to interpret the great Italian classic of the nineteenth century to a wider public in this country than those who can approach him in the original.

It has been my aim in this translation that it should not be in the remotest sense a paraphrase, but far rather a faithful and a close, though not servile, rendering of the original. Hence I cherish the hope that it may not prove useless to students of the Italian language in enabling them to elucidate the intricacies and difficulties of Leopardi's style and language.

Of the thirty-four *canti*, ending with *The Genista*, that last and most mature and most sublime product of Leopardi's genius, I have omitted three from this translation; two (*Consalvo* and the *Palinode*) as being likely to seem of little interest or even trivial to English readers, the third (*On the Marriage of My Sister Pauline*) as being, though fine in itself, mainly repetitionary of the lofty sentiments and of the fervour and passion of Leopardi's other patriotic odes. The desire not to swell too much this small volume was also of weight with me, and may prove, I hope, my exoneration from reproach.

I have retained Leopardi's form and metre, employing the same regular, and sometimes intricate, sequences of rhyme wherever he does. Leopardi, however, latterly almost discarded this artificial aid to verse, as if it were a base fetter which impeded the free soaring of his genius. But as more frequent rhyme seemed essential to our less plastic and less musical northern tongue, I have ventured to increase the number of rhyming lines where the poet used such irregularly and sparingly, as, for instance, in *The Genista*.

The numbers in parenthesis above the titles of the poems indicate the sequence of the latter in the Italian edition.

J. M. MORRISON.

CONTENTS

I

TO ITALY

My native land! thy walls I still behold,
Thy arches, columns, monuments, and waste
Lone towers our fathers manned;
But not thy glory, nor
The laurel and the sword with which of old
Our sires were girt, I see.   Now thou defaced,
With naked brow and barèd breast, dost stand.
Ah me! thy wounds so sore,
Thy pallor and thy blood!   Oh, woeful plight
Of thee, thou lady fair!   Ye earth and air,
O tell me, I implore,
Who brought her down so low?   And, viler sight,
That both her arms with fetters should be bound,
So that she sits unveiled, with loosened hair,
Hiding her face between her knees, forlorn
And desolate, on the ground,
And all disconsolate weeps.
Weep, Italy; right well thy tears may flow,
Who'rt other nations born
To excel in thy prosperity and woe!

But though thine eyes were e'en two living springs,
Thy tears could ne'er atone
For all thy ignominy and thy shame,
Who sovereign lady wast, but now art slave.
Who speaks of thee, or sings?
Who that recalls thy glorious past, now flown,
But says : 'She once was great—is this the same?'
Alas! why is it so? Where are thy arms,
Thy steadfastness, thy worth, thy strength of old?
Who wrenched from thee thy blade?
Who was it thee betrayed? What art or charms,
What might or power so bold
Thy cloak and golden bands from thee to take?
How art thou fallen? Who made
Thee stoop from such a pinnacle to shame?
Does no one fight for thee? Bring arms!
A sword! Alone I'll fight and die for thee!
Grant that my blood enflame,
O Heaven, Italian breasts to dare be free!

Where are thy sons? I hear men's shouts, the
　　clash
Of arms, the noise of wheels, the trumpet flare.
In foreign lands afar
Thy children battle wage.
Hark, Italy! I see, methinks, the flash
Of swords, as through the mists the lightning glare,
And swaying horse and foot in throes of war,
And smoke and dust o'erhead.
Does't please thee not? Those trembling eyes of thine

Dar'st thou not to the doubtful issue bend?
Why on these plains is shed
Young Italy's rich blood? Ye powers divine!
For other lands Italians hurl their spear.
O hapless wight who warring meets his end,
Not for his fatherland, and for his wife
Beloved and children dear,
But at the hands of foes
Of foreign States, who, dying, cannot say,
'Sweet country mine, the life
Thou gav'st me, lo, to thee I now repay!'

   O fortunate, and dear, and blessed age
Of old, when heroes rushed
In serried ranks to die for fatherland,
And ye, Thessalian passes, high enrolled
In history's glorious page
Of fame, where fate and Persia's might were crushed
By that small band of warriors noble-souled!
Methinks each rock, and brook, and blade of grass,
And mountain there, with whispering secret boast,
To travellers must relate
How buried all along that mountain pass
Lies that unconquered host
Of victims, given to Greece an offering.
Then, full of shame and hate,
Across the Hellespont King Xerxes speeds,
To's children's children made a laughing thing;
And up Anthela's hill, where in their death
That sacred army deathless life did gain,

Simonides proceeds,
And scans the earth and air and ocean's main.
And, down his cheeks fast trickling bitter tears,
With tottering steps and palpitating breast,
He grasped in's hand his lyre :
Of blessed memory ye,
Who offered free your breasts to foemen's spears,
For love of your dear land at her behest ;
Ye whom Greece honours, and all men admire !
To perils of the fray
What wondrous love your young hearts did beguile?
What love did drag you to your bitter doom?
Brave sons, how seemed so gay
That latest hour to you, that with a smile
Ye to death's tearful bourne and cruel sped?
It seemed that to the dance, and not the tomb,
Or to a splendid feast, ye all were bound :
But you the waters dead
And Tartarus did await;
Alas ! to none was wife or children near,
When on the fatal ground
Ye died without a kiss, without one tear.

But not without the Persians' awful moan,
And loss and dire despair.
As lion midst a herd of bulls at bay
Now springs upon the back of one, and now
With's teeth lays bare the bone,
And now that flank and now that thigh doth tear,
So midst the Persian ranks infuriate play

Greek swords, and valorous, strong right arms fierce
    fight.
See horse and rider bite the dust and die,
See fallen tents and wains
Impede the beaten foe's inglorious flight ;
And midst the first to fly
The tyrant, woe-begone, bewildered, pale.
Barbarian blood, lo, stains
Greek hands and brows, and dripping from them runs
With havoc fell the Persians they assail,
Till, overcome by wounds and loss of blood,
They rear aloft the glorious pile.   All hail !
All hail ! ye blessed ones,
As long as men shall sing or say this tale !

   The stars upwrenched and in the ocean thrown
Shall sooner hiss, extinguished in the deep,
Than fade away or pall
Your memory and your fame.
Your tomb an altar is, where shall be shown
By mothers to their little ones that weep
Sweet stains of your rich blood.   Prostrate I fall,
Ye blessed, on the ground,
And humbly kiss these rocks and earthy clods,
Whose glorious praise from pole to pole shall live
And evermore resound !
Ah ! were I with you there, and might these sods,
So sacred, by my blood be turned to ooze !
If fate decrees this not, and will not give
That I the light that fills these trembling lids

In war for Greece may lose,
Some modest fame yet may
Your bard amongst posterity secure,
If Heaven this not forbids,
Which shall, like yours, till time's no more, endure.

II

ON THE MONUMENT TO DANTE

THOUGH Peace, as with a pall,
Her snow-white pinions round our country wraps,
Italian breasts shall ne'er
Shake off their ancient heavy slumber's thrall,
Unless the spirit of our sires of yore
Imbue this land, a prey to dire mishaps.
O Italy, to thee
Be't dear to honour thy great dead ! thy land
Seems reft of such to-day for evermore,
And none is fit to honour now thy name !
Look backwards, O my fatherland, and see
Those great immortal names' infinite band,
And weep and of thyself think bitter shame ;
For what can grief avail without shame's thrill ?
Turn thee, awake, and of thyself feel scorn !
Let our sires' mem'ry fill
Thy heart and thoughts of ages yet unborn !

The stranger of a different genius, clime,

And tongue, the Tuscan land once wandered thro',
If haply he might learn
Where *he* lay dead whose song was so sublime
That now the bard Mæonian has a peer,
And heard (O shame on you !)
Not only that in ban of stranger earth,
Since that lugubrious day,
His bleached bones lay and ashes cold and sere,
But not within thy walls one stone did stand,
O Florence, to him for whose sterling worth
All men thee honour pay.
O happy ye, such foul disgrace with hand
So leal to wipe away from this our land !
Let all whose breasts with love of Italy burn,
Ye courteous, valiant band,
With love this noble deed ye've done return !

Dear ones, to you be given
Poor Italy's love to bid your task godspeed !
For her in every breast
Pity seems quenched for aye, since on us Heaven
Has, after sunshine, evil days bestowed.
Take heart the more, her sons, and let your deed
By pity now be crowned,
By grief and anger at such sore distress,
For, see, her cheeks with tears are overflowed !
But with what wealth of word or song ought we
To honour you for ever now renowned,
Not only for your care and thoughtfulness,
But for the genius and the skill which ye

In this dear scheme have shown of brain and hand?
What words shall I address to you to fire
Your heart, as with a brand,
And with a spark divine your soul inspire?

 Your lofty theme shall inspiration prove,
And with keen goads your ardent souls impel.
Who shall express the flood
And passion of your zeal and boundless love?
The frenzy of your mien inspired, your eye
Keen flashing who shall tell?
What mortal words a subject so sublime
Can ever hope to paint?
Far off, all ye profane!   O Italy,
The tears upon this noble stone thou'lt shed!
How shall your glory fade, or how shall time
With gnawing tooth its lustre mar or taint?
And you by whom our woes are lightenèd,
Ye arts divine and dear, live ye for aye,
Our ill-starred race's consolation sole,
Intent in her dire day
Of ruin, Italy's high praise to extol!

 I too with ardour strong
Our doleful mother to revere desire,
And bringing what I may,
I mingle with your labour this my song,
Here where your chisel shall make marble live.
O thou of Tuscan song illustrious sire,
If word may reach that land

Where thou immortal dwellst, of earthly thing,
Of her to whom thou deathless fame didst give!
I know for thine own sake this cannot thee
Elate, for no more firm than wax or sand,
Compared with thine undying glory's ring,
Are bronze and marble!   If thy mem'ry we
Have e'er forgot, or do nòt ever keep,
Let our misfortunes grow, if they can grow,
And let thy country weep,
By all despised, in everlasting woe!

   I ask thee not to joy for thine own sake,
But thy poor country's, if each noble deed
Of sires and grandsires e'er
In their sons' torpid breasts degenerate wake,
Such valour that once out the dust they rise!
Alas! thou seest her bleed
With how long torment, who so poor and mean
Saluted thee that day
When thou didst mount again to paradise!
Now brought so low (her depths thou dost perceive!),
That matched with this she seemed a prosp'rous queen.
To such woes she's a prey
As thou, amazed, perchance canst not believe.
Her other foes and evils I pass by,
But not her latest and most direful one,
By which thy land well-nigh
Saw o'er her ruined gates set her last sun.

   O blessed thou, by grace

Of fate, who didst not see such horrid woes,
Nor Italy's fair dames
Beheldst in barbarous soldiers' foul embrace ;
Nor yet her ruined towns and fields a prey
To hostile spear and rage of foreign foes ;
Nor sawst dragged far and wide
Beyond the Alps her works of art divine
To vile captivity ; nor yet the way
All tearful with dense rows of waggons blocked ;
Nor mark'dst the rude commands and despot's pride;
Nor heardst the insults and the impious whine
Of that word ' Liberty ' which grossly mocked
Us mid the stroke of lash and clank of chains.
Who grieves not ?   What have we not borne ?   Vile
    crew !
Ye've left no altars, fanes
Undesecrate ! no deed's too foul for you !

   Why saw we such degenerate days depraved ?
Why didst thou give us birth, or why not dower
Us first with boon of death,
O cruel Fate ? who, though thou sawst enslaved
This land of ours to foreign, impious yoke,
And mordant file devour
Her utmost strength, no comfort didst bestow,
Nor stretch a helping hand
The bitter, anguished grief, which nigh did choke
Her very life, in some small way to bate.
Alas ! we gave not life, nor yet did flow
Our blood for thee, dear land,

Nor did I die to avenge thy direful fate!
Hearts swell with pity deep, with anger hot!
Full many of her children drew their swords,
And fought and fell, but not
For dying Italy—for tyrant lords!

    Father, if such woes rend
Thee not, thou'rt not he once on earth thou wast!
On the Ruthenian plains
All barren died (alas! worth nobler end)
The Italian brave, and on them air and sky
And men and beasts waged bloody war and vast.
They fell in squadrons dense,
Half-naked, stained with gore, and worn and pale,
And on a couch of snow they sick did lie!
Then when they bore their latest agony,
'Remembering their dear Mother with intense
Desire, they cried: 'Would not by wind and hail
And rain we'd died, but by the sword for thee,
Our native land! From thee untimely torn,
When fairest smiles upon us youth's heyday,
Abandoned and forlorn,
We perish for that land which thee doth slay!'

    Across the wintry waste their plaintive cry,
And o'er the rustling woods, was piteous borne—
So came they to their doom,
And their abandoned bodies 'neath the sky,
Upon that awful snow-besprinkled sea,
By ravenous beasts were torn;
And aye the names of these brave men and true

Shall be in one same page
Enroll'd with cowards and dastards!   Yet rest ye
In peace, brave hearts, altho' your grief and pain
Be infinite ; let this thought comfort you
That neither in this age
Nor in a future shall ye comfort gain!
Upon the bosom of your boundless woe
Sleep ye in peace, leal sons of her whose last
Misfortune's fatal blow
Not even by your dread doom can be surpassed!

For this your country heaps
Reproaches not on you, but him who drove
You 'gainst her to contend,
So that she bitterly for ever weeps,
Mingling her tears with those upon your cheek.
O might pity for her whose glory throve
Above all others' give
One of her sons such goads that from this dark
And deep abyss he'd drag her forth, all weak
And worn and frail !   O glorious spirit, say,
Does love of Italy no longer live?
For aye is quenched thy deep devotion's spark?
Shall never more grow green that laurel bay
Which long was wont to alleviate our smart?
Are all our chaplets scattered on the floor?
Shall none who in some part
Resembles thee arise for evermore?

Are we for ever lost, and for our shame

Shall limit ne'er be found?
I, while I live, to all shall loud proclaim :
' Turn to thine ancestors, degenerate race ;
Gaze on these ruins round,
These volumes, temples, painters', sculptors' art ;
Think of what soil thou treadst, and if the glow
Of such ensamples cannot fire thy heart,
Why waitst thou ?—rise and go !
This land, the fost'rer of great souls, not meet
Can be for such a vile, degenerate brood ;
If't be of cowards the seat,
'Twere better far it lone and widowed stood !'

III

TO ANGELO MAI

ON HIS DISCOVERING CICERO'S 'DE REPUBLICA'

THOU bold Italian, wilt thou never cease
To summon from the tomb
Our sires, or tire of luring them to teach
This age nigh moribund, sunk in the gloom
Of slothful lethargy?   How now doth reach
So oft and so appealing to our ears
Our fathers' voice that slept
These many centuries?   Why all these new
Renaissances?   Quick as a flash of light
The frequent parchments come.   Till these our years
The dusty cloisters kept
The sacred, lofty sayings from our view
Our fathers wrote.   Does Fate thee with hid might
Inspire, O great Italian, or amain
Fights Fate perchance with human might in vain?

It cannot be without Heaven's deep design
That when our sad neglect
Had reached a hopeless stage, and most severe,

Each moment on our ears should strike direct
Some new voice from our sires.   To Heaven still dear
Is Italy ; still to our need some blest
Immortal's head is bowed.
This hour Fate now or never doth allot
To us to show the old Italian worth
Grown rusty in our breast.
Let's see, then, since so loud
The dead appeal to us, and long forgot
Great heroes seem at length laid bare by the earth,
If 'tis, O fatherland, thy fitting part
At this late age to play the craven heart !

O glorious ones, do ye retain some hope
Of us ?   Are we not left
To ruin dire?   To you 'tis not forbid,
Perchance, to read the future.   I, bereft
Of hope, no shield have 'gainst despair, since hid
To me's the future, and so vile appear
All things, that hope but dream
And madness seems !   Ye souls of deathless fame,
Your seats a graceless, shameless race has found
Its home.   All strength of word and deed but jeer
And jest your seed doth deem.
Your deathless praise evokes no blush of shame
Nor envy more.   Vile sloth doth now surround
Your monuments, and our degeneracy
A thing of scorn to future times shall be.

Illustrious scholar, when none else a thought

To our old sires doth give,
Thou thinkst of them—thou whom Fate doth inspire
So bounteously, that once more seem to live
At thy behest those days* when from their dire
Oblivion old upreared their lofty head,
With Learning erst entombed,
The ancient seers, with whom Nature conversed,
Her veil unraised, on whom the festive crowd
Of intellectual Rome and Athens fed.
O times, eternal doomed
To sleep! Not yet was Italy immersed
In ruin dire; her sons were still too proud
To sink in base inaction, and the wind
Could still some sparks to fan in this soil find.

Thy sacred ashes scarcely yet were chilled,
Thou Fortune's dauntless foe,†
To whom, heart-sick with scorn and misery,
E'en hell more kind than earth herself did show!
E'en hell! Can any lot more hellish be
Than this our life? Thy lyre's harmonious strings
Sweet whispering yet did thrill
From thy soft touch, O lover‡ sore oppressed
By woes! Alas! Italian song arose
From pain. And yet less fatal is the sting
Of gnawing, dolorous ill
Than stifling slothfulness. O thou all blessed,
Whose life was tears! Whereas our swaddling-clothes

* The Renaissance period.   † Dante.
‡ Petrarch.

2

Disgust has girt, and Nothingness calm sits
Beside our crib, and o'er our tomb she flits.

But thy life then was with the stars and sea,
Liguria's daring son,*
When out beyond the Pillars and the shore
Which seems to hear waves hiss, when dips the sun
At eve, thou, launched into the infinite roar
Of waves, didst see the sunk sun's ray-crowned head
Once more, and find the day
Which dawns when ours into the dark has flown;
And, Nature's every obstacle surpassed,
A new and boundless world did lustre shed
Upon thy voyage, and way
Back into risks.   Alas! the world when known
Not waxes, but doth wane, and far more vast
The earth and sea and sounding atmosphere
To little children seem than to the seer.

Where are our pleasing, dearly-cherished dreams
Of the sequestered seat
Of unknown peoples, or the slumber deep
Of stars by day, or the far-off retreat
Of youthful, rosy dawn, or nightly sleep
Of great Sol's mighty orb, securely hid?—
All fled, all vanity!
The world is figured on a tiny chart;
Lo! all things are alike.   When all's laid bare,
The Nothing only grows.   Thou dost forbid

* Columbus.

Us, loathed Reality,
Sweet Fancy's fairy realms.   From them doth part
Our mind for aye ; from their stupendous, rare,
Ephemeral sway us soon withdraw our years,
And fled is our one solace in our tears.

Thou,* meanwhile, for sweet dreams wast born,
        and thy
Youth's sun shone full and clear,
Delightful singer of love's might and arms,
Which, in an age than this of ours less drear,
Existence filled with fond delusion's charms.
New hope of Italy, O cells, O towers,
O noble dames and knights,
O gardens, palaces ! I think of you,
And in a thousand vain, delightful thrills
My soul ecstatic sinks.   This life of ours
Was full of fair, vain flights
Of foolish dreams !   In ban we did pursue
Them.   What is left when first the Real chills
The charm of things ?   The certainty remains
Alone that all is vain except our pains.

Torquato, O Torquato ! Heaven was then
To thee but woeful wrong
Preparing, but for us thy mind sublime.
O wretched Tasso ! vainly thy sweet song
Essayed to comfort thee, or thaw the rime
Wherein the hate and petty, envious sneer

* Ariosto.

2—2

Of men thy heart encased,
Which once so warmly throbbed.   That last deceit
Of this our life forsook thee—even Love !
Substantial shape the Nothing did appear
To thee, the world a waste
All lone and drear.   Thine eyes did never greet
Thy tardy honours' fame ;* not loss did prove
Thy latest hour, but gain.   He claims but death
Who knows life's ills, and not a laurel wreath.

   Return to us once more ; return, and quit
Thy mute and cheerless tomb,
O luckless sport of Fate, if still are dear
Life's agonies to thee !   Our present doom
Is viler far than that which seemed so drear
And all unblessed to thee.   O dear, sweet bard,
Who'd now lament thy fate
When only of himself is each one's care ?
Who would not laugh to scorn the woes that thou
Endur'dst, to-day, when gibes and jeers reward
Each spirit choice and great ;
Nor envy more, but—far more hard to bear—
Indifference befalls the great ?   Who now,
When money-bags, not song, the world command,
Would give the laurel-crown into thy hand ?

   From thy time, ill-starred genius, to this hour
But one who by his birth
Sheds lustre on the Italian name came forth,

* Tasso died whilst preparations were being made to
crown him *more antiquo.*

Of whom his coward age was all unworth,—
Fierce Allobrog,* whose breast the hardy north,
And not this worn-out, arid earth, did fire
With manly valour's might ;
Whereby, unarmed and single-handed, he
(O wondrous daring !) 'gainst the tyrant gang
Waged ruthless war.   At least, to fruitless ire
Of men let this vain fight
And miserable warfare solace be.
He first alone into the arena sprang,
And none did follow him, for sloth and ease,
Befitting slaves, our torpid breasts now freeze.

In proud disdain and righteous rage he spent
Unstained his whole life-time,
And death from fouler sight did him remove.
O Victor, this was not the age or clime
For thee !   Another time and land behove
Men of heroic mould.   Content we've found
In sloth, and all are led
By mediocrity.   The mob has sprung
To one dead level with the fallen sage,
And all are like !   Discov'rer wide-renowned,
Go on !   Awake the dead,
Since we, the living, sleep !   Fire each mute tongue
Of ancient heroes, that at length this age,
Earth-bound and vile, may catch life's quickening
    flame,
And rise to noble deeds, or blush with shame !

* Alfieri.

IV (5)*

TO THE VICTOR AT TENNIS

BE 't thine to know, O youth of generous blood,
The siren voice and smile
Of fame, and how superior manly zest
Is to effeminate sloth.   Rouse thee awhile,
Stout-hearted champion, if from the flood
Of rushing years thy valorous soul would wrest
Renown's eternal prize—rouse, rouse thee, stir
Thy heart to high resolves !   To glorious deeds
Invite thee echoing arena and
The applauding circus crowd's loud buzzing whir ;
Thee, joyous in thy youth, thy fatherland
Beloved equips to-day
The deeds of ancient heroes to display.

Not he in the barbarian blood did steep
His sword at Marathon
Who, on Olympus' plain, at athletes stripped
For contest arduous, like boor looked on ;

* The figures in parenthesis refer throughout to the
number of the piece in the Italian edition. (*See* Preface.)

Nor did the envied palm and wreath, so deep
Desired, e'er fire his blood.   Perchance they dipped
In pure Alpheus' stream the dust-stained flanks
And manes of their victorious steeds—those men
Who Grecian standards and Greek lances bore
Amid the panic-stricken, pallid ranks
Of worn and routed Persians : whence a roar
Of baffled rage rang o'er
Euphrates' lofty breast and servile shore.

Is their task futile who reveal and fan
The dying ember glow
Of nations' strength, and who revive again
In fainting breasts the fervour, burnt so low,
Of the ebbing vital spark ?   Since Phœbus 'gan
To roll his mournful wheels, are the acts of men
Aught but an idle farce, and is less vain
The truth than falsehood ?   Nature to our aid
Joy's phantom forms and sweet deceptions sent :
And when long use unbounded and insane
No sustenance more to strong delusions lent,
Its high pursuits of fame
The world exchanged for barren sloth and shame.

The time may come when desecrating flocks
O'er crumbling piles shall stray
Of Italy's renown, and boors up-plough
Rome's seven hills ; few years shall roll away,
Perchance, before his hole the wily fox
Shall fix in Latin states, and groves shall bow

Their shaggy, rustling tops o'er their proud walls;
If Fate does not remove that deadly, dire
Neglect from out the hearts of perverse men
Of this our country's weal, and Heaven recall
Not her heroic past and smile again,
And from an abject race
Avert not ripe disaster's threatening face.

Be't grief to thee, good youth, thy country's dead
Renown to have survived!
Thou wouldst have won for her a deathless fame
When flashed her crown, of which she's now deprived
By guilt of ours and Fate's.   These times have fled;
And none reveres now such a mother's name:
Yet be thy valiant soul to heaven uprist!
What does our life avail—save for contempt?
Blest only when thro' danger's shoals she steers,
Oblivious of herself, and does not list
The flood and gauge the flight of moulding years;
Blest only when, the brink
Of Lethe reached, then on her charms we think!

V (6)

THE YOUNGER BRUTUS

WHEN now Italian chivalry, laid low
In dire destruction, bit
The dust of Thrace, and for the verdant meads
And vales of Italy, and Tiber's banks
Fate now the tramp of the barbarian steeds
Prepares, and summons from those forest wastes,
Banned in the frozen north,
The Gothic hordes to crush Rome's might, against
Her walls imperial hurled :
Then Brutus, bathed in sweat and in the blood
Of's countrymen, amid night's gloom alone,
Now bent on death, the Fates and nether world
Inexorable doth chide,
And with shrill words and fierce
In vain the quivering, drowsy air doth pierce.

  O frenzied valour, 'tis the empty clouds
And restless phantoms' fields
That are thy schools, and gaunt remorse doth stride
Behind thy steps ! Ye marble-hearted gods !

(If ye indeed in Phlegethon reside,
Or 'bove the clouds), to you a laughing-stock
And gibe is man's sad race,
From whom ye temples claim; and men a law
On trickery based doth jeer.
Does then terrestrial piety excite
Celestial hate so far? dost thou protect,
Jove, impious men? and when storm-clouds career
Along the heavens, and thou
Thy rapid bolt dost flash,
Thy sacred fire 'gainst just and good dost dash?

Indomitable destiny and iron
Necessity oppress
Death's helpless slaves : the mob, if not so strong
As make their insults cease, this thought consoles,
That ills are necessary.   But is wrong
Less cruel that's irreparable?   Feels he
Not pain who's lost all hope?
War to the death and bitter end, O Fate
Unblessed, the brave who know
Not how to yield do wage with thee; and aye
Thy tyrant hand which, conquering, lays them low
They shake triumphant off with dauntless show,
When they the fatal steel
Plunge in their breast within,
And greet the gloomy shades with hideous grin.

They who to Hades force their way displease
The gods.   In dastard breasts

Divine could courage such as this ne'er move.
Perchance these playful gods our toils and pains,
Bitter experiences and ill-starred love
Decreed as sport unto their leisure hours?
A free life in the woods
And innocent, not fraught with guilt and ills,
Had Nature for us found,
Goddess and Queen awhile. Now that from earth
A godless use that blessed state has driven,
Our stunted life to other laws she bound.
When life's unenvious lot
Our manly souls refuse,
Does Nature us of the rash stroke accuse?

All ignorant of guilt and of their wrongs,
Wild beasts more fortunate,
To 'ts bourne all unforeseen serenely drag
Their lingering age. But if they dash their heads
'Gainst gnarled stem, or from some mountain crag
To cast themselves headlong into the air
They should be urged by pain,
No secret law, or hellish spirit, born
Of darkness would contest
Their miserable desire. Alone on you
Amongst all beings God-create, alone
Of all, Prometheus' sons, has life hard prest!
Ye wretches! Hades' realms,
If coward fate have grown
Too hard, Jove doth forbid to you alone.

And thou, pale moon, arisest from the sea

That blood of ours doth dye ;
Thy searching beams the night unpeaceful flood,
And that field fatal to Italian might.
The conqueror tramps on foe of kindred blood,
The hills bewail the Rome of old down hurled
From her proud pinnacles ;
And canst thou rest so calm ?   Thou sawst the birth
Of the Lavinian race,
Her fadeless laurels and her glad, proud years ;
And thou thy changeless, peaceful beams wilt shed
Upon the Alps, when, mid the vile disgrace
Of Italy enslaved,
Beneath barbarian feet
Shall loud resound that solitary seat.

Amid the branches green and barren crags,
With torpid breasts that bode
No daily care or ill, lo ! bird and beast
Nought of that ruin proud, or of the world's
Poor transient glories know : when from the east
The ruddy dawn the toiling peasant's cot
First lights, the birds will wake
The vales with morning song, and beasts of prey
O'er precipices the breed
More feeble of the lesser beasts will hunt.
O fates !   O luckless race ! the abject part
Of things are we ; our woes have ne'er been heed
Unto the blood-stained soil,
Or caves of moaning wail,
Nor have the stars thro' human pains grown pale.

Not I Olympus' or Cocytus' kings
Stone-deaf invoke, nor yet
Base earth, nor dying night, with piteous wail ;
Nor thee, last hope to which the dying cling,
Praise of posterity !   Can sobs avail
To appease proud tomb ; did ever deck it words
And gifts of rabble vile ?
The times are out of joint ; degenerate sons
Are but a broken reed
Whereon to hang the honour of great minds,
And last revenge of wretched souls.   Her wings
Round me let flap the boding bird of greed ;
Let beasts devour, and clouds
Bear off my dust obscure ;
My name and mem'ry let the air secure !

VI (7)

TO SPRING

OR

ON ANCIENT FABLES

Whereas the sun repairs
The winter's havoc, and the languorous air
Is stirred by quickening breeze which drives the
    banks
Of ponderous, lowering clouds in scattered flight,
And birds their bosoms bare
Commit unto the wind, and sweet sunlight
Inspires the deep-stirred beasts with new desire
Of love, new hope, whilst it their forest dens
Deep penetrates, and melts the winter snows ;
Perchance their vigour shall return to men's
Grief-sunk and wearied hearts
Again, which sorrows and the hateful torch
Of stern reality
Untimely sapped.   Not Phœbus' rays alway
Are then withdrawn from wretched man, and quenched
For him ? and dost thou too,
O fragrant Spring, thy soft touch tempting lay

Upon my frozen heart, which in the bloom
Of youth's heyday learns age's bitter doom ?

   Blest Nature, dost thou live
Indeed ; dost live, and on the unwonted ear
Fall the maternal accents of thy voice ?
Erst streams and crystal fountains were the calm
Resorts and mirrors clear
Of beauteous nymphs.   Mysterious dance of feet
Immortal made the tottering ridges thrill,
The lofty woods to quake—to-day the bleak
Abode of winds : the shepherd who was wont
His thirsting lambkins leading, once to seek
The unearthly flitting shapes
Of noon, and rivers' flowery margins, heard
The rustic train of Pan
Shrill pipe along the banks ; and saw the wave
Soft quiver, and stood awed when now Dian,
Fair huntress, all unseen
Descended to the tepid flood to lave
The grimy dust of the ensanguined chase
From her pure virgin breast and snow-white face.

   The flowers, the grass, the woods
Were living beings once.   The breezes light,
The clouds, and Phœbus' orb held sweet converse
With men ; and once the traveller, with gaze
Intent in dead of night
Pursuing thee, disrobed fair Venus, Star
Of Eve, along the uplands and the hills,

Imagined thee his consort by the way,
Solicitous for men.　Or he who fled
The base society of towns, the play
Of deadly strife, and shame,
Withdrew into the forest depths and clasped
To 's breast the shaggy stems,
And thought that through their bloodless veins there
　　　thrilled
A living fire, and breathed their leaves, whilst sad
Phyllis and Daphne 'neath
A loathsome embrace trembled, awed and stilled ;
And hapless Phaëthon wept unconsoled,
Whom Helios in Eridanus deep rolled !

　Nor did the piteous wail
Of human anguish strike unheard your ear,
Ye firm-set rocks, whose awesome, lurking caves
Were haunts of solitary Echo once—
She who was not a mere
Vain phantom of the air, but the hapless shape
Of some sweet nymph, whom unrequited love
And cruel fate held disembodied.　She,
Mid grots, bare crags, and desolate abodes,
Poured forth to heaven's blue vault such misery
Herself had known, and our
Loud, sobbing plaints.　And fame reported thee
Expert in human ills,
Sweet, tuneful bird that from the leafy bowers
Now celebratest Spring's return with song,
And from thy rural, high

Retreat, unto the air that stilly lowers,
Our ancient ills and vile disgrace dost wail,
And daylight's face with rage and pity pale.

   But not akin to ours
Can thy race be ; not pain e'er teaches thee
Thy varied notes ; the gloomy valley hides
Thee far less dear than man, but yet guilt-free.
Alas, alas, since void
Are heaven's courts, and blind the thunderbolt
Along the darkling clouds and mountains strays,
And just and unjust equally with fear
And shrinking smites ; and since the natal soil,
Estranged and heedless of her own, doth rear
A sad and weakling race ;
Do thou, sweet Nature, heal the bitter cares
And the ignoble fate
Of mortal man, and to my breast restore
The ancient fire ; if only thou dost live,
And there is aught in heaven,
Or on this sunlit earth, or 'bove the floor
Of ocean that one glance of *interest* throws—
I dare not say of *pity*—on our woes !

VII (8)

HYMN TO THE PATRIARCHS

OR, ON THE PRIMITIVE HUMAN RACE

YE sires illustrious of the human race,
Your sad ill-fated sons shall ever sing
Your praises forth !   Far dearer you than we
To the eternal Urger of the stars,
And far less tearful was your fate than ours
Beneath day's bounteous light.   Not love divine,
Nor just Heaven's law doomed wretched man to
    woes
Incurable ; nor yet pronounced the curse
That he be born to tears, and find the grave's
Dark portals and the gloom of death more sweet
Than heaven's ethereal light.   And if the old
Sore wail be true that through your ancient sin
Man's race became a prey to the tyrant might
Of fell disease and ills, yet 'twas your sons'
Far direr misdeeds, and their restless souls,
And boundless folly that against us roused
Heaven's outraged ire, and the despisèd hand
Of bounteous Nature ; whence the fevered fret

Of life, and issue from our mother's womb
Pressed heavy on us, and on earth emerged
The dark despair and doom of Erebus.

Thou first didst gaze upon the light of day,
The empurpled torches of the wheeling spheres,
The new-created denizens of the fields,
And heard the zephyrs o'er the virgin lea
Soft sigh, first Guide and Parent of our race:
What time the mountain torrents headlong beat
With yet unwonted roar upon the rocks
And lonesome valleys; when mysterious peace
Reigned calmly o'er the blissful future seats
Of nations far renowned, of busy hum
Of cities vast; when Phœbus' bounteous rays
And Luna's golden beams, so lone and still,
The untilled uplands climbed. O blessed thou,
Earth's solitary seat, all inexpert
In sins and dire mishaps of fate! What woes,
What bottomless abyss of bitterest ills,
O wretched Father, Heaven is brewing now
For thy unhappy seed! Lo, fury unknown
The thirsting furrows first pollutes with blood
And fratricidal butch'ry, and the sky's
Blue vault first sees the accursed wings of Death!
The fear-urged fratricide now roams the earth,
And flees the dismal shadows, and the winds'
Mysterious rage within the forest depths,
And grim, gaunt care finds shelter and a throne
First 'neath the roofs of men; and now too first

Despair's remorse, all wan and gasping sore,
Unites man's helpless race in social bonds
For mutual refuge and retreat ; whereby
The impious hand did spurn the curvèd plough,
And rustic toil was counted vile ; and sloth
In scoundrel halls now reigned supreme ; and,
    quenched
The native vigour of enervate frames,
Now minds lay fallow, sluggish ; and mankind
In craven bondage—that last ill—was sunk !

And thou didst poor, ill-fated creatures save
From threatening skies and watery waste that surged
Around the cloud-capped peaks, O thou to whom
The milk-white dove from out the brooding gloom
And from the emergent summits emblem bore
Of hope restored, when now the sinking sun,
Long flood-immersed, forth issuing from the clouds,
Set radiant bow athwart the gloomy sky.
The rescued race revisits earth once more,
And now resumes its savage passions' play,
Its impious pursuits, with all their woes
And fears attendant.   Now with hand profane
They foully violate the trackless realms
Of the avenging sea, and to new shores
And other worlds impart their ills and plaints.

Of thee, O Father of the faithful, strong
And righteous now I meditate, and those
Illustrious scions of thy race !   How thou
Beneath the shelter of thy shady tent

Wert seated at noontide, beside the folds
And soft luxuriant pastures of thy sheep, ·
When unawares celestial spirits came
In stranger guise and blessèd thee; and how,
Astute Rebecca's son, at eventide,
Beside the rustic well and in the glad
Retreat of Haran's valley, sweet resort
Of shepherds, thou wert smitten sore with love
Of Laban's lovely daughter—boundless love
Which led thy dauntless spirit to endure
Without one murmur hardships and exile
And hateful yoke of bondage many years.

There was a time—nor does Æonian song
And glory's voice seduce the greedy crowd
With vain delusions' phantoms—when this land
So hapless was propitious to our race,
And dearly loved; and when the age, alas!
Decadent now, was named of Gold. 'Twas not
That torrents undefiled gushed from the rocks'
Maternal breasts in milk, or with the sheep
The tiger laid him down in common fold,
Or that the shepherd led the frisking wolf
To lap the spring; but heedless of his fate
And inexpert in ills man lived, and still
Exempt from cares; the dear deceptions, sweet
Delusions—kindly veil of pristine days
O'er Heaven's and Nature's laws mysterious thrown—
Still reigned supreme; her sails swelled high with hope,
Our peaceful barque calm glided into port.

Amidst the Californian forests vast
Such race is born, whose breast no pallid care
Doth gnaw, whose limbs no wasting, lingering, fell
Disease devours ; the forest yields them food,
The cavern depths a shelter, drink provides
The copious watered valley, death's dark doom
All unforeseen o'ertakes them.   O ye realms
Of sapient Nature all defenceless 'gainst
Our impious daring !   Our unbounded lust ·
And madness desecrates all coasts and lairs
And virgin woods ; it teaches ravished tribes
Anxieties unfelt before, desires
Unknown ; and chases from her last retreat
Felicity, a naked fugitive !

VIII (9)

SAPPHO'S LAST SONG

THOU night serenely calm, and thou chaste light
Of downward sinking moon, and thou from out
The peaceful wood that climbst above the cliff,
Day's messenger; O apparitions dear,
Delightful to mine eyes, while yet unknown
To me were Fate's avenging Furies! now
No sweet, fair scene arrides my love-rent heart.
Through us joy, unaccustomed yet, doth thrill,
When from the south the dust-beladen winds
Swift roll along the liquid air, and sweep
Across the swaying fields, and when the car
Of Jove deep thundering o'er our head doth cleave
Its heavy path along the lowering sky.
We love to float amid the rain-charged clouds
Across the crags and valleys deep, and hear
The panic-struck stampede of herds, the sound
Of swollen river fell
And treach'rous, or the waves' resistless swell.

Most fair thy vesture, sky divine, and thou

Most fair, O dewy earth !   Alas ! the gods
And ruthless Fate to luckless Sappho give
No share in this their beauty infinite !
Rejected lover, vile and grief-bowed guest,
Devoted to thy proud and lofty throne,
I turn in vain, O Nature, pleading heart
And supplicating eyes to thy most sweet
And gracious charms.   For me there is no smile
In sunny slope, or morning light of dawn
Fresh stepping from the gate of Heaven ; not me
The song of gaily plumaged birds, or beech
Soft whisp'ring, greets ; and where the silvern stream
Doth bare her radiant bosom 'neath the shade
Of willows bent to kiss, her sinuous waves
From underneath my slippery feet she draws
In proud disdainful slight,
And hugs her odorous banks in speedy flight.

  What grievous fault, what so accursed crime
Polluted me in prior birth that now
Heaven's face and Fortune's thus should frown on
      me ?
What was my sin as babe, those years when life
No evil knows, that now the iron thread
Of my existence reft of youth, deflowered
Of joy, should round the spindle fast be whirled
Of all-unconquerable Fate ?   But hush !
Thy lips but utter reckless words : and Fate's
Decrees aye through mysterious counsels move.
All save our pain is mystery.   To woes

Our god-forsaken race was born ; the why
Lies hid in Heaven's lap !   O cares, O hopes
Of our young years !   Eternal empire gave
The Father to illusions over men—
Illusions sweet.   To bards' clear lyric lays
And noble, valiant deeds
Lovers who've ceased to charm no virtue leads.

We die.   Its veil ignoble flung aside,
The naked soul shall wing its flight to Dis,
And mend the cruel blunder of the blind
Dispenser of the Fates.   And thou to whom
Long hopeless love, long loyalty and rage
Of unappeased desire me vainly bound,
Be happy, if e'er mortal man on earth
Lived happy yet !   Me Jove besprinkled not
With that sweet liquid from the niggard cask,
When that the dreams and the delusions died
Of my young years.   The happiest days
Are those that from our life first fleet away.
Disease, old age, the ghost of icy death
Creep on apace.   Lo, now there waits for me,
Of all those sweet delusions and desired
Rewards, but Tartarus !   My valiant soul
Enshroud for evermore
The Stygian flood, black night, the silent shore !

IX (10)

FIRST LOVE

I well recall the day when love first came
And thrilled my heart, and I thus made lament :
'Alas ! if this be love, how fierce his flame !'

My eyes aye fixed upon the ground intent,
I stood amazed at her who first did show
The way unto my heart still innocent.

Ah, love ! thou dealt'st me such a cruel blow !
Why must so sweet affection bring along
With her such fierce desire, such bitter woe?

Why not serene, and pure, and free, and strong,
Instead of mixed with grief and pain's alloy,
Did so much rapture in my breast upthrong?

Tell me, my gentle heart, what dread annoy,
What anguish sore was thine amid the thrill
Compared with which but sorrow was each joy?

That thrill that did beguile by day thy will
And in the night thee of thy rest did rob,
When all the earth seemed wrapped in slumber still.

Thou sweet, yet sad, restless like surging mob—
I tossing on my couch—didst throng my breast
Which all the while tumultuous did throb.

And when I sad and tired and grief-oppressed
My eyelids closed, then came, like sleep that flies
By fever and delirium broke, my rest.

How vivid in the darkness did arise
That image sweet, and how too I did dote
Upon it, as I lay with closed eyes !

Oh what delightful, sweetest thrills did float
And creep along my bones ! how vex and tease
My mind a thousand thoughts that did denote

Nought but was vague, confused ! as zephyr breeze
Sweeps thro' the foliage of some ancient grove,
And makes a long, weird moaning 'mong the trees.

And whilst I silent lay, nor 'gainst them strove,
What didst thou say, sad heart of me, when she
Was going, whom it throbbed for, sick with love ?

No sooner did I feel love's flame in me
Fast boiling o'er, than that soft breeze, I found,
Which served to counteract the heat, did flee.

Sleepless I lay, till day once more came round ;
The steeds, about to take from me all hope,
Stood at my father's door and pawed the ground.

I timid, silent, all unused to cope
With love, strained in the dark a greedy ear
To the balcony, my eye in vain wide-ope,

To catch her voice, if I some word might hear
Fall from her lips—the last, ah, who could tell!
Since Heaven denied all else that I held dear.

How oft plebeian voices cheerless fell
On my expectant ear, my blood too froze,
My heart at random 'gan to throb and swell!

And when at last her dear words did repose
Within my heart, and sound of hoofs, and glide
Of wheels upon my listening ear arose;

Like one whose life's a blank, I quivering hied
Me to my couch again, and clutched my heart
With fevered hand, and closed my eyes and sighed.

My tottering knees I then, with cruel smart
Distraught and dazed, dragged through my chamber
　　　stilled;
' Now Fate,' I cried, ' has spent her last fell dart !'

Most bitter, then, the memories that thrilled
My breast, and every voice and form seemed vain
Unto my grief-sore heart, all stark and chilled.

My bosom long was racked with searching pain,
As when from heaven the rain in ceaseless pour
Monotonously falls and floods the plain.

I did not know thee, love, a boy no more
Than twice nine summers old, and who was born
For tears, too, when thy first assault I bore.

When, too, I treated every joy with scorn,
Nor cared for smile of stars, or green array
Of fields, or silence of calm, rosy morn.

And love of glory now no more could sway
My breast, with which 'twas wont so fierce to burn,
When love of beauty came therein to stay.

My eyes to old pursuits I could not turn,
And books and studies now seemed vain to me,
For which all longing else I used to spurn.

Alas ! how could I e'er so changed be,
And other love from me such strong love take?—
How altogether vain in truth are we !

My heart was my one joy, and I did make
Communion deep with it in one long strain,
And scanned my pain, like sentinel awake.

My eye aground in introspective train
Of thought I kept, nor let it fleeting light
With wayward glance on comely face or plain;

Because it feared that stainless image bright
To desecrate, which did my heart enthral,
As lake is stirred by breeze, however slight.

And that remorse not to have tasted all
My joy, with which our souls are oft depressed,
That pleasure, too, which, faded, turns to gall,

Through those past days continually oppressed
My bosom, though not yet had Shame demure
Her cruel teeth in this my heart impressed.

I Heaven and all ye gentle souls adjure
To know my breast ne'er harboured base desire,
But burned with unpolluted fire and pure.

Still that affection lives, still lives that fire,
That image fair still fills with bliss my mind;
It never did but holy joy inspire ,

In me ; in it alone content I find.

X (11)

THE SOLITARY THRUSH

O LONELY thrush, sad thou dost sit and sing
In rustic spot upon the top of that
Old tower, until the daylight dies away ;
Whilst harmony throughout the valley reigns,
Around, the joy of spring
Is in the air, blithe tripping o'er the plains,
And at the sight each heart doth rapturous beat.
Hark to the lowing kine, the flocks that bleat ;
All other birds together gaily vie,
As wheeling thro' the air they dart and fly,
Seeming with joy to greet the season fair ;
Thou seest it all apart, as full of care ;
And, still, with ne'er a friend
Car'st not for mirth and shunst each glad pastime ;
Thou singst, and so dost spend
Thy years' fair season and thy life's young prime.

   Alas ! how like appears
Thy nature, bird, to mine ! Mirth and pastime,
Those dear, sweet comrades of our youthful years,

And thee, O youth's twin brother, love, sad sigh
And keen regret of hoary age's rime,
I care not for, I know not why; nay, far
From them I seem to fly ;
And, like a stranger lone
In's native place, forlorn,
I let my life's young springtime glide away.
This day about to fade into the dark
Is in our town an annual holiday.
Hark in the air a sound of bells, and hark
The frequent thunder of discharge of guns,
Which far from house to house re-echoing runs !
The youth, too, of the town,
In festive garb beclad,
Come out of doors and scatter up and down,
To observe and be observed, so spruce and glad.
All solitary I,
Postponing each delight
And pastime to some other hour, my eye
The while by the ardent glare
Dilate, am dazzled by the sun which sinks,
After the day so bright,
Behind the distant hills, and seems to say
That my sweet youth, too, quickly fades away.

　　Thou, lonely bird, when thou hast reached the end
Of such life as the stars thee may allot,
Wilt certainly not grieve
O'er these thy ways, since each desire of thine
From Nature only springs.

But I, if I may not
Avoid the hated brink
Of lingering, crabbèd age,
When's dimmed the light which fills these eyes of mine,
And earth's a blank, and when each day aye more
And more annoy and gloom than that before
Will bring, what shall I think
Of these desires and years of youth ?   Repent
I often shall my life,
But, hopeless aye, my thoughts be backward bent.

XI (12)

THE INFINITE*

Dear ever to my heart that lonely hill
 Hath been, that hedge, too, which extending wide
 The view of farthest horizon doth hide.
Here as I sit and muse, my thoughts at will

Do summon scenes of boundless space behind,
 Of silence passing human ken, and rest
 Unbroke, unfathomèd, whereat the breast
In awe doth well-nigh sink ! And when the wind

I hear surge through the rustling leaves that sway,
 I aye compare its whispers with that all
 Pervading silence deep, and I recall
Eternity, and ages passed away !

* It is with much misgiving that I offer this rhymed
version, which may seem like tampering with Leopardi's
sublime blank verse. My only apology is that the rendering of this gem was the first I attempted, and that it was
made before I had any idea of translating more. As my
attempt still seems to me accurate enough at least, I
retain it.—*Translator.*

The present lives, and all its stress with me,
  Howe'er. Thus in the boundless Infinite
  My fancy sinks, like drowning man from sight—
How sweet to suffer wreck on such a sea !

XII (13)

EVENING OF A FESTIVAL

THERE'S not a breath disturbs the calm, clear night,
Whilst mid the gardens and above the roofs,
The pale moon stands, revealing from afar
Each mountain-top serene.   O lady mine,
Each lane is hushed in silence now, and rare
In balconies the night-lamp flickers faint,
But thou dost sleep that gentle sleep which closed
Thine eyelids in thy quiet rooms ; no cares
Disturb thy rest ; no heed or thought hast thou
Of that sore wound thou'st piercèd in my breast.
Thou sleepst : I, standing at my window, greet
The bounteous sky so clear which meets my gaze,
And Nature, too, omnipotent of old,
Which formed me for annoys.   'Hope I deny
To thee,' she said, 'aye, even hope ; and nought
But tears shall light thine eyes for evermore !'
To-day was festival ; now thou dost rest
From thy pastimes ; perchance rememberest
In dreams how many thou to-day didst please,
How many pleasèd thee · I have no hope

That I shall come into thy thoughts.   Meanwhile,
I ask how long I still must live ; I throw
Me on the ground, and groan, and weep.   O life
In my young years so loathed !   Alas ! I hear
At hand, along the road, the mournful song
Of artisan who hies at dead of night
From his festivities to's humble home ;
I feel my heart in wild convulsion beat
To think how all within this world doth pass,
And leave scarce trace behind.   This holiday
Is gone, and after festival succeeds
The common daily round, and time bears oft
Of men's lives each event.   Where's now the sound
Of those old nations ?   Where is now the fame
Of our illustrious ancestors, and Rome's
Imperial might, her arms, and their loud clang
Resounding world-wide over sea and land ?
Ah ! silent all, and all that world doth lie
Oblivion-sunk, their glory but a name !
In my young years, what time we eagerly
Look forward to the festive day, so soon
As it was o'er, I vigil kept, and clutched
My couch in pain, and at the midnight hour
In such wise did I feel my heart grow cold,
When I a like song heard along the lanes,
Which slowly in the distance died away.

XIII (14)

TO THE MOON

SWEET, graceful Moon ! I still remember well
How I, with anguish torn, one year agone,
Returned across that hill to gaze on thee ;
And thou wert floating then above that wood,
As thou art now, and flooding it with light.
But to my sight thy countenance appeared
All bleared and tremulous with bitter tears
Which filled mine eyes ; for life to me was grown
A burden, and still is, nor evermore
Can cease to be, O Moon beloved ! And yet
That memory's dear, and to recall mine hours
Of pain doth bring me joy. Oh sweet, in time
Of youth, when hope's track still lights far ahead,
And memory's course is but begun, presents
Itself the recollection of the past,
Though sad, and sore with pain's enduring sting !

XIV (15)

THE DREAM

'Twas early morn, and through the shutters closed,
Along the balcony, the sun's first rays
Soft stole their way into my sombre room ;
When at the hour that Sleep now lays her hand
Most lightly and most gently on our lids,
Before me rose and flashed upon my gaze
The form of her who first did show to me
The way of love, and then left me to tears.
Not dead she seemed but sad, and in the guise
Of some disconsolate semblance.   On my head
She placed her hand, and heaving sigh profound,
She spoke : ' Dost live, and still retain of us
Some memory ?'   I answered : ' Whence and how
Com'st thou, dear Sweet ?   Alas ! how deep
My grief for thee once was and is ; yet I
Ne'er thought that thou shouldst learn it, and 'twas
      this
My grief the more inconsolable made.
But say thou wilt not leave me once again :
'Tis that I dread.   Say what has thee befallen :

Art thou she once I knew ?   What secret ill'
Gnaws at thy heart ?' 'Forgetfulness,' she said,
'Enshrouds thy thoughts and sleep beclouds thy mind ;
For I am dead, and 'tis some moons ago
Since thou didst see me that last time.'   At these
Sad words profoundest grief oppressed my heart.
'Cut off in my youth's flower,' continued she,
'Was I, when life is fairest, and before
My heart had learned the lesson how man's hopes
Are wholly vain.   'Tis surely not amiss
A pain-racked wretch should long for death which rids
Him of all woes ; but cheerless 'tis when death
O'ertakes youth's prime, and cruel is the fate
Of hope extinguished in the dank, cold tomb.
All vain is knowledge such as Nature hides
From those in life's ways yet unskilled, and blind
Unreasoned grief doth wield a potent sway
O'er wisdom all unripe.' 'Unhappy one,
And dear,' I cried, ' no more ! Thou rendst my
   ·   heart
With these thy words !   Art thou then dead indeed,
Beloved, whilst I still live ? and was it then
In heaven decreed that thy dear, tender frame
Should prove the agony supreme, whilst I
Should keep unscathed this wretched mortal coil
Of mine ? Alas ! how often when I think
That thou'rt no more, and how it may not be
That I e'er meet thee in this world again,
l cannot deem it true ! Alas ! what is
This thing called death ? Oh, might I learn by proof

To-day what 'tis, and my defenceless head
Withdraw from Fate's most cruel, vengeful shafts !
Full young I am, but yet, like hoary age,
Is wasted and consumed my youthfulness ; *Concept of Heaven.*
Old age I dread, while yet 'tis far away,
And yet 'twixt it and my youth's prime but slight
The difference is.'   ' We both were born,' said she,
' To tears ; no smile of happiness has blest
Our lives ; our woes have been the sport of Heaven.'
I answered then : ' If thy departure caused
Mine eyes to fill with tears, my cheeks to waste
With sickly pallor, and my heart to swell
With heavy anguish, say, oh, say, did e'er
A spark of love or pity, whilst thou liv'dst,
Thy heart enkindle for the hapless wretch
Who loved thee so ?   I, 'twixt despair and hope
Alternate, then dragged out each day and night,
Till now with vain expectancy my heart
Lies bruised and worn.   Oh, if e'en once thou felt
A spark of pitying grief for my sad life,
I pray thee hide it not !   The thought will bring
Me healing balm, since hope's denied to us
All time to come.'   She answered: ' O poor wretch,
Be comforted !   I did not thee deny
My pity whilst I lived, nor do I now,
For I was wretched, too.   Oh, bear no grudge
To me, a poor forlorn, unhappy maid !'
' By our misfortunes,' I exclaimed, ' that love
That, wasting, me undoes ; by that beloved
Sweet name of youth, and by the blighted hope

Of our existence, grant, O dearest one,
That I may touch thy hand!'　With gesture sweet
And sad she held it forth, and whilst I it
With kisses smother, and with panting joy
And rapture, blent with pain, it madly strain
Unto my heart, great beads bedewed my brow;
My fevered bosom throbbed, my voice was choked
Within, the light danced 'fore my reeling eyes.
Then, fixing tenderly her eyes on mine,
She spoke : ' Dear heart! hast thou indeed forgot
Already that of beauty I am reft,
And all in vain, O wretched wight, thou burnst
And thrillst with love?　And now, in fine, farewell!
Our miserable souls and bodies must
Be sundered evermore.　To me thou'rt dead,
And nevermore shalt live.　The troth thou pledg'dst
To me is snapped by Fate.'　Then I essayed
To shriek with anguish, and awoke from sleep
With spasms cruel torn, my cheeks all bathed
In bitter, anguished tears.　Her shape still swayed
Before mine eyes, and in the flickering light
I seemed to still behold her phantom form.

XV (16)

THE SOLITARY LIFE

THE morning shower awakes me, pattering soft
Upon my window-pane, what time the hen,
Flapping her wings upon her snug roost-perch,
Loud cackles, and rustic dweller anxiously
Peers o'er his balcony, and when the sun,
Now rising, darts his dancing, tremulous rays
Amid the gently downward-falling drops ;
I rise and greet with benisons the light
And filmy clouds, the early twittering song
Of birds, the fresh soft air and smiling meads ;
For long enough you have I seen and known,
Ye hated city walls, wherein go hand
In hand both hate and pain ; where painfully
I live, and so shall die—may Heaven grant soon !
At least some scrap of pity Nature shows
Me in this spot—she who was once so much
More kind to me !   Even thou too turnst thy face
From wretch's cry ; and thou, O Nature, all
Misfortunes, sufferings disdaining, fawnst
On Queen Felicity.   Thus nor in heaven

Nor earth is any friend or refuge left
To wretched man except the kindly steel.

   Sometimes I seat me in some lonely spot
Upon an eminence near by the shore
Of lake bediademed with flowers unstirred.
There, when the zenith sun has climbed the heaven,
He glasses on its bosom his calm face,
And not one breath a leaf or blade doth stir;
No ruffle on the water's breast, no chirp
Of gay grasshopper, and no flutter mid
The trees of wings, or buzz of butterfly;
No voice or motion far or near I hear
Or see. Profoundest peace reigns o'er these shores,
Where I, ne'er stirring, as oblivious
Of self and all things, sit; methinks e'en now
My limbs are froze in death, nor feeling more
Nor breath of life in them; their primal peace
Confounded with the silence of the scene.

   O Love! O Love! full long thou from my heart
Hast been estranged, which once did glow with such
Impassioned heat. Misfortune's clammy hand
Has chilled it now, and in my youthful prime
'Tis turned to ice. I still recall the day
Thou first didst storm my breast. It was that sweet,
Irrevocable time when first the view
Of this world's vale of tears before the gaze
Of young man opes, and smiles on him like some
Fair scene of paradise. His youthful heart

Within his virgin breast beats high with hope
And vague desires, and now the luckless wretch
Himself for life's stern battle girds, as if
For dance or play equipped.   But not so soon,
Love, knew I thee; already on Fate's wheel
My wretched life was broke, and nought beseemed
Mine eyes but everlasting, bitter tears.
Even if at times along the sunny slopes
I meet the gaze of some sweet maiden fair
At peaceful rosy dawn, or when the hills
And fields and housetops sparkle in the sun;
Or oft as in the calm serene of some
Soft summer night my wayward straying steps
I stay before some village home, and gaze
Upon the desolate ground, and hark the full
Clear song resounding through the lonely rooms
Of maiden, who prolongs her household toil
Into the night; my stony heart then starts
To beat convulsively: alas! it soon
Returns to its dull, heavy sleep; for all
Sweet thrills have stranger grown to my steeled breast.

Beloved moon! beneath whose soft calm light ·
Hares gambol in the woods, and at the dawn
Of day the huntsman grieves who finds the tracks,
Misleading from the lairs, all intricate
And false and blurred; all hail, auspicious Queen
And kindly of the night!   Unwelcome fall
Thy beams through thickets, or deserted house,
Or mid the rocks, upon the dagger-blade

Of trembling highwayman, whose straining ear
Doth catch the noise of horses and of wheels
Still in the distance, and the tramp of feet
Upon the lonely road ; caught unawares,
The traveller then doth feel his blood run cold
At noise of arms, hoarse voice, and muffled face
Confronting him, and soon half dead and stripped
Is left upon the ground.   Unwelcome falls
Thy soft, pale light amid the city streets
Upon the vicious gallant, who along
The walls of houses closely slinks, and keeps
Deep in the shadow, and stands still, and cowers
In terror at the brightly-blazing lamps
And open balconies.   Unwelcome, too,
To guilty conscience is thy face, but dear
To me will be aye in these scenes, where nought
But smiling hills and spacious fields e'er meet
My gladdened gaze.   So, too, it was my wont,
All innocent, to lay it to the charge
Of thy sweet light, when in the haunts of men
Thou offeredst me to human gaze, and when
I saw the face of man before mine eyes.
So thee I'll ever praise, when I behold
Thee floating mid the clouds, or when, serene
And sovereign lady of the ethereal plains,
Thou lookst upon this human vale of tears.
Thou oft wilt see me silent and alone
Stray through the woods, and by the green-clad shores,
Or seated on the sward, well satisfied,
If I have heart and breath to heave a sigh.

XVI (18)

TO MY LADY

DEAR sweet, who me with deep,
Strong love inspir'st, although thy face thou hid'st,
Save that 'fore me in sleep
Thou, fair as heaven, vague glid'st ;
Or in the fields when shines
Most fair the day, and Nature sweet doth smile ;
Perchance that Age men call
The Golden thou didst bless, which knew no guile,
But now on earth dost flit
A phantom soul?   Or hides thee niggard Fate
From me, reserved for men of later date ?

  To see thee in the flesh
I may no longer hope,
Unless it be when, naked, stripped, and lone,
My soul shall wing its flight o'er tracts unknown
To'ts new abode.   Even when at first did ope
My earthly sojourn, dark, and vague, and drear,
I thee upon this barren waste did deem
A wanderer.   But nought on earth doth seem

To be like thee, and even if aught thy peer
Could be in speech and action, form and air,
'Twould still, thus like to thee, be far less fair.

   Amid so much sore pain
As Fate to mortal life here doth allot,
Should one on earth love thee, fair as I feign
Thee in my thoughts, and as thou really art,
Blessèd would be life's lot ;   .
And well I know that praise and virtue still
From thee outflow, such as in my young years
Thy love conferred on me.   Now Heaven accords
No comfort to us in our woes and tears ;
With thy sweet presence life on earth would flow
In rapture such as the immortals know.

   Along the valleys, where
The toiling peasant's song is echoing borne,
I often sit and mourn
My youth's illusion, which me now forsakes;
And up the hills, where I recall and weep
O'er my now lost desires, the vain, lost hopes
Of my young days, my pulsing heart awakes
To thrill with thought of thee.   And may I keep
In this dark age and this accursed air
Thy lofty image ! for with thy image vain
I'm pleased, who may not see thyself again.

   If thou be one of the old
Eternal Thoughts, who, as with bonds, dost scorn
To clothe thy Sense Eternal with the things

Of sense, and, in earth-born
Frail frame of dust imprison'd, know the tears
Of death-sad life ; if other earth in spheres
Supernal, mid unnumbered worlds, thee hold ;
If of our sun a sister star more fair
Illume thee, and thou breathe a kindlier air ;
O hence, where few and evil are life's days,
From unknown lover take this hymn of praise !

TO COUNT CHARLES PEPOLI

How fares with thee this fever'd, anxious dream
Which we call life, dear Pepoli? What are
The hopes wherewith thou vainly still buoyst up
Thy heart? In what deep thoughts, or what routine
Of tasks, pleasing or onerous, immersed,
Dost thou fulfil thy leisured hours, that hard
And irksome heritage bequeathed to thee
From thy far ancestors? Yet life itself
Is nought but leisure in all human lots,
If deed and forethought, striving after aim
Unworthy, or that never may attain
Their goal, can fitly be named leisure. If
The hardy sons of toil, whom peaceful morn
And eve behold tilling the soil, or plants
And flocks attending, thou shouldst designate
As leisured, since their life's an effort but
To bear with life, which in itself to man
Is nothing worth, thou wouldst say truth. His days
And nights the sailor spends in leisure; toil
Unceasing in workshop, and bivouacs,

And watches, and war's risks but leisure are.
In leisure grasping, greedy merchants live,
For none by care, or sweat, or watch, or risk
Attains for self or others happiness—
That sweet, illusive bourne for which alone
Our mortal nature strives and yearns. To soothe
That bitter craving after bliss, for which
Mankind has ever sighed in vain, since first
The world sprang into being, Nature has
Provided for our wretched life, by way
Of remedies, divers necessities,
Which we could never hope to satisfy
Without forethought and toil, and in the search
For which our years might glide full occupied
At least, if they could not be happy ; so,
That restless passion, thus diverted, dulled,
Might cause our heart less travail. Thus brute beasts'
Prolific offspring, in whose breasts there lurks
Alone, nor less than ours, that futile, vain
Desire for happiness, intent on what
Shall furnish them life's necessaries, finds
Time less oppressive and less sad than we,
Nor chides the lingering passage of the hours.
But we, who the provision of our wants
To others' hands commit, may not discharge
Without disgust and pain a far more dire
Necessity, for which none can provide
Save us, to wit, the stern necessity
To endure life's pilgrimage : that impious,
Invincible necessity, from which

Not hoarded treasure, nor abounding flocks,
Not fruitful fields, nor gilded halls, nor robes
Of purple can dispense our race.   Should one,
Scorning the empty years, and hating heaven's
Pure light, refrain his suicidal hand
To turn on self, though urged to anticipate
His lingering fate, he 'gainst the cruel sting
Of that vain craving, irremediable,
For happiness, by searching on all sides,
Provides a thousand ineffectual cures,
Which illy compensate for that sole one
That Nature has put ready to his reach.
He, then, devotes his life to train and curl
His locks, and to attain due elegance
Of garb, and port, and gait, or to vain quest
Of steeds and equipages, or frequents
The crowded drawing-rooms, the fashionable
Promenades and public gardens, nightly feasts,
The gaming tables and the envied dance.
A laugh ne'er issues from his lips, alas !
But in his inmost breast broods deep, firm-set
As adamantine column, *ennui* vast
And quenchless, 'gainst which wrestles, all in vain,
Youth's vigour, and which soft accents of love
From rosy lips, and tremulous, tender glance
Of dark-eyed maid—sweet glance, that earthly thing
Most like to the divine—can ne'er assuage !

Another, as if bent to flee man's lot
So sad, will spend his years in visiting

Strange lands and climes, and, wand'ring over hills,
And vales, and seas, will traverse all the earth,
Subduing the utmost limits of such space
As Nature deigns in the infinite realms
Of the universe to man. Alas ! black Care
Broods o'er the lofty prow, and all in vain
Is happiness invoked beneath all climes
And skies, and only sadness reigns supreme.

  Some, too, select the cruel art of war
To while away their years, and dip their hands
In brothers' blood to kill the time, and some
Take comfort in their neighbour's harm, and think
By rendering others miserable to make
Themselves less so, thus dragging out their years
By injuries. Some eke the allotted span
In the pursuit of arts and sciences,
Or virtue ; some in trampling down their own
Or foreign people, or in ravishing
The ancient peacefulness of shores remote
With trading, and with arms, and fraudulence.

  But thee a gentler fire, a sweeter care
Sways in thy youthful bloom, thy years' most fair
April, to all else chief, delightful gift
Of Heaven, but bitter, hostile, onerous
To him who owns no country. Thou art moved
And stirred by love of song, and zeal to extract
The rare, elusive, fleeting beautiful
In the universe, and that which fancy sweet,
And our own dear illusions, kindlier far

Than Heaven and Nature, bounteously produce
In us.   Ten thousand times, yea, is he blest
Who in the flight of years abandons not
The transient, perishable potency
Of sweet imagining, on whom the fates
Bestowed the boon to keep his heart aye young;
Who in his virile and decrepit age,
As was his wont when in his youthful prime,
In's inmost thought doth Nature beautify,
And life to death and desert gives.   Heaven grant
To thee such fortune !   May that spark divine
Which now inflames thy breast make thee in years
To come sweet Poesy's hoar wooer still !
All fond delusions of my early years
I feel already dead, and from mine eyes
All faded those loved images which I
Once held so dear, which, till my latest breath,
I shall recall with yearning sighs and tears.
Then when to all around this breast of mine
Is steeled and dead, and now no more the smile
Serene and lonely of the sunny fields,
Nor sweet at early morn the song of birds
In spring, nor more along the hills and dales
Beneath the calm, clear sky the silent moon
Shall move my heart ; when now to me all art
And Nature's beauties shall be dead, nor find
Response in me ; each lofty sentiment,
Each tender feeling, be unknown and strange ;
I, beggared of my only solace, then
To other less sweet studies shall devote

The unlovely remnant of my unblest years.
Then bitter, stern reality I shall
Investigate, the blind, hid destinies
Of mortal and eternal things ; why man
Was made, why weighted with a load of cares
And miseries ; towards what final goal
May Fate's decree and Nature's urge him ; whom
That endless pain of ours delights or boots ;
By what order and laws, and why revolves
This enigmatic world, which sages heap
With praise, but I'm content to wonder at.

In speculations such as these shall I
Drag out my leisure ; for the *real* known,
Though it be sad, has charms.   And if, when I
Thus reason on the real oft, my words
Prove unaccepted or unheard of men,
'Twill grieve me not, for that old raging thirst
Shall long ere then in me be quenched for Fame—
That goddess who's, besides being wholly vain, ·
More blind than she of Fortune, Fate, or Love.

XVIII (20)

THE RESURRECTION

I THOUGHT in me indeed,
Ere yet my youth had fled,
Those sweet, sad pains were dead.
Felt in my early years :
   Sweet tears and tender thrills
That in the heart have birth,
Whatever on this earth
Our life with pleasance cheers.

   Ah me ! the plaints and tears
In my new life outburst,
When from my froze heart first
That sweet, sore pain did fly !
   Gone were my ancient throbs,
Me love no more opprest,
My steeled and bruisèd breast
Did e'en forget to sigh !

   I wept that life for me
Was stark and barren made ;

The sterile earth was laid
In endless icy tomb ;
    The day desert; more lone
And dark the silent night;
No moon my way did light,
The stars were quenched in gloom.

    Still of my plaint the cause
Was love's sad wound of yore :
Within my bosom's core,
Deep down, yet beat my heart.
    My wearied fancy called
Those images beloved
Of old ; my sadness proved
But ancient grief and smart.

    And soon that latest pain
In me was even spent,
No longer to lament
Had I the strength e'en left.
    No comfort did I seek ;
Like a dead log I lay :
My lifeless heart gave way,
As lost and hope-bereft.

    Such was I !—how unlike
Him in whose soul did beat
Once such impassioned heat,
And wayward dream of love !

The wakeful swallow who
The gabled eaves along
Doth chirp her morning song,
My heart *she* could not move :

Nor e'en the vesper bell,
What time comes Autumn sere,
In manor lone and drear,
Nor sun at close of day.
In vain Eve's Star I saw
Shine o'er the hedgeway still,
And nightingale did trill
Grovewards her plaintive lay.

And stolen glances ye,
In melting wayward eyes,
Thou love that never dies,
Thou gentle swain's first'love ;
And thou, white naked hand,
In mine so coyly laid ;
In vain have ye essayed
My torpid breast to move !

Though sad, yet undismayed,
With countenance serene,
And calm unruffled mien,
Of every joy bereft ;
I might have prayed for death
To bring me glad relief ;
My heart all worn with grief
Had not one prayer left.

As if with clammy hand
Decrepit age did cling
So soon to me, the spring
Thus of my youth I spent:
 Thus, heart of me, thou livedst
Those days divinely sweet,
To us, so short and fleet,
By niggard Heaven lent.

This dull, lethargic sleep
Who bids me shake at length?
What is this new-born strength
I feel in me expand?
 Ye fancies, thrills, and throbs,
And yearnings vague of youth,
Are ye not then in truth
My heart for ever banned?

Are ye my life's unique
And only guiding star;
Those loves that from me far,
New-born, I did dismiss?
 From heaven, and each green field,
Where'er I turn mine eyes,
Everywhere sorrow sighs,
Everything whispers bliss.

Once more I feel I live
With shore, and woods, and hills;
My heart doth list the rills,
I hark the whispering sea.

Who gives me anew my tears,
So long from me estranged,
How does the world seem changed,
Where'er I look, to me ?

Poor heart of me, kind hope
On thee did smile perchance ?
Ah, no ! kind hope's sweet glance
On me no more shall smile.
Nature gave me my thrills,
And sweet delusion's throes ;
In me was lulled by woes
My native strength awhile ;

But not destroyed : not it
Could fate or ill subdue ;
Nor she of loathsome hue,
Hateful reality.
I know my fancy's dreams
And she stand far apart ;
That Nature steels her heart,
And hears not wretch's cry.

I know existence was
Her only care, not weal :
That we be broke on the wheel
Of fate is her one heed.
I know that in this world
No pity e'er abides ;
That elusive it derides
Our every mortal need.

For genius and virtues all
This sordid age cares not;
Contempt is still the lot
Of every lofty aim.
And you, my trembling eyes,
And thou, my gaze divine,
I know in vain ye shine—
Not you doth light love's flame.

Yours is no sentiment
That's lofty or divine:
That placid breast of thine
No love-born spark e'er guards.
At others' tender cares
She's ever wont to jeer;
And ever with a sneer
The fire divine rewards.

But yet I feel revive
Those old delusions' snares;
My breast her throbs and cares
Regards with wondering awe.
That inborn fire of me,
O heart, and this last sigh,
And every solace I
From thee alone must draw.

Though I earth's beauty all
And joy must ever lack,
Though Fate and Nature rack
My pure and lofty mind:

Still if thou liv'st, O wretch,
Nor yet fate's victim fall,
Her I will never call,
Who gives me breath, unkind.

XIX (21)

TO SILVIA

My Silvia, canst thou still
Recall that period of thy life now gone,
When in thy bright eyes shone
Soft beauty's witching, laughing, wayward glance,
And thou hadst just begun, so coyly gay,
To enter youth's heyday?

Once all the lanes around,
And gloomy rooms with thine
Unceasing song did sound,
Whilst thou upon thy woman's work intent
Wouldst sit, thy mind content
With that bright future which thou dreamtst for thee.
It was the fragrant May, and thus thy days
Without one care did flee.

Then leaving my loved books
And studies over which I used to pore,
And spend the sweetest time
Of my young days, my listening ears stretched o'er
The balconies of my father's castle, I

Drank eager in the sound of thy sweet voice,
And as thou spanst, I watched
Thy nimble hand the busy wheel deft ply.
I gazed the while on sky
So clear, the golden lanes
And gardens, distant sea and nearer hill.
No mortal tongue can tell
What bliss my breast did thrill !

What sweetest thoughts, what hopes,
What heavenly strains were ours, my Silvia dear !
How fair did then appear
The life of man and fate !
When I recall these hopes so high, I feel
My heart disconsolate
Weighed down with bitterness,
And life's sad woes my spirits sore depress.
O Nature ! Nature ! say
Why dost thou not fulfil
The promise of those years ?   Why thus betray
Thy sons with so much ill ?

Thou, ere the warm spring sun did sear the grass,
Attacked by secret malady and laid low,
Didst perish, O sweet child !   Thou didst not know
The flower of thy best years ;
Thy heart ne'er felt the joy
Of homage sweet to thy dark hair, nor, 'bove
Thee bending, love-lit glances' tribute coy ;
Nor did thy comrades e'er on holidays
Commune with thee of love.

So my sweet hopes did die,
Like thee, in one brief space; so too the fates
Did youthfulness deny
Unto my years.   Alas! is this,
Is this then thy sad end,
O thou to my young days the dearest friend,
My sore lamented hope?
Such is the world.   Is this
The love, the deeds, ambitions, this the bliss
Whereon together we so oft communed?
Poor child, thou at command
Of stern reality didst pass; thy hand
Did from afar point out the cheerless tomb
And ice-cold death—our doom!

XX (22)

MEMORIES

FAIR Ursa's stars, I did not think to gaze
Upon you ever, as of yore, again,
Bright glittering o'er the trees around the old home,
And from the windows of the manor, where
As boy I lived, and saw the end of all
My happiness, to commune sweet with you.
What fancies and what vain conceits the sight
Of you and of your sister stars once stirred
Within my breast, the while I used to sit
In silence on the verdant sward, and spend
Long stretches of the evening hours, my gaze
Fixed on the sky, my ears intent to catch
The distant croak of frogs across the fields !
Along the edges and amid the grass
The glow-worm trailed her lamp, and in the wind
Soft whispered perfumed avenues and groves
Of cypress-trees ; alternate voices smote
Mine ears, and sound of peaceful, household toil
Of menials from indoors.   What boundless realms
Of thought, what reveries sweet spread 'fore my mind's
Horizon that far-distant sea, those peaks

That tower into the azure sky, and which
I hoped one day to pass, mysterious worlds
And joys thus shaping for my destiny !
Not knowing what Fate held in store, and how
I many a time would soon desire to change
My miserable and barren life for death.

My heart ne'er whispered to me I should be
Condemned to spend my youth's best years in this
Rude, savage country town where I was born,
Amongst a boorish set of men, to whom
The name of learning and of knowledge is
An empty word, and often, too, their butt
For mirth and jeers ; who hate and shun me, not
Because they envy me, for they hold me
No better than themselves, but just because
They think I deem myself such in my heart—
Not that I ever gave them cause for this.
Here spent I all those lifeless, loveless years,
Forlorn, misunderstood ; and, mid that folk
Unfriendly, I perforce rude, churlish grew.
Here I all piety and virtues lost,
And learned to be a scorner of mankind
Through contact with this herd.   And meanwhile fled
The precious days of youth, more precious far
Than laurel crown or fame, more than the pure,
Sweet light of day, or breath itself.   In this
Inhuman habitation, midst annoys,
I squandered thee away without one joy,
O thou the only flower of dreary life !- *youth*

Hark ! from the town-house tower the wind doth
     bring
The sound of striking hour. I well recall
What comfort brought to me that sound of nights,
When, as a boy, in my dark, gloomy room
I lay awake, with haunting terrors racked,
And sighing for the morn. Here not one thing
I see or feel but to my mind recalls
Some faded image, some sweet memory brings—
Sweet in itself ; but yet the present, fraught
With pain, will creep into my thoughts—a vain,
Sad yearning for the past, the knell—Thou'st lived !
That balcony there, which catches the last light
Of fading day ; those walls all covered o'er
With pictured cattle, and the rising sun
Across the lonely scene, all offerèd
My leisure hours a thousand joys, the while
I with my vivid, wayward fancy held
Sweet commune evermore. And whilst outside
The snow bright sparkled and the wind round those
Bay-windows howled, along these ancient halls
My child-play and bright prattle echoed loud,
What time the unwelcome, bitter mystery
Of things presents itself to us wrapt up
In kindly veil. Like lover all unskilled,
The boy doth shyly gaze upon and make
Sweet eyes at his untarnished, spotless life,
And, heavenly beauty feigning it, admires.

O hopes ! O yearning hopes ! delusions sweet

Of my young days ! I ever hie me back
To hold commune with you. ¶ You through the flight
Of years, through all my changing loves and thoughts,
I never can forget.   Methinks that fame
And honour are but dreams, all bliss and joys
Mere vain desires _ Life has no flower or fruit,
All's hopeless misery !   And though my years
Are barren all, although my destiny
Is lone, obscure, full well I know that me
Of little Fortune robs.   But when, alas !
I think of you, my ancient hopes, and thee,
Thou first, sweet, fond imagining of mine,
And then perceive my life so vile a thing
And grievous, and that death alone is all
That's left to me to-day of so much hope,
I feel my heart grow cold ; I feel that I
Shall never more find comfort in my fate.
And when at last death, long invoked, shall take
My hand, and I have reached the goal of life's
Sad pilgrimage ; when earth to me has grown
A stranger land, and time to my tired eyes
Shall be no more for aye, you then indeed
Shall I remember, and that image still
Shall haunt me mid my sighs, and bitter make
The thought of life so vainly lived, and mar
The sweetness of my latest day with pain.

   Already in the conflict of my youth's
First days 'twixt pleasures, agonies, desire,
I often called on death, as, seated there

Long hours upon the fountain, I did brood
Of ending all my hopes and all my pain
Within its crystal depths.   Thereafter brought
By malady mysterious to death's door,
I wept my youthful bloom so fair, the flower
Of my sad days which so untimely drooped.
And oft as, seated on my abetting couch
At midnight hour, I scribbled painfully
My verses with the aid of lamplight dim,
Amid night's gloom and silence I bewailed
My fleeting breath, and, sorely languishing,
I sang unto myself a dirge-like song.

Who can without a sigh remember you,
O portal of youth's pleasant morn, O days
Of sweet, ineffable delight! when first
The witching maidens bend their sweetest smiles
On raptured swains, when everything around
Doth vying smile, and envy's tongue is still,
Or if it wags is kind, and, so to speak,
The world (O marvellous, unwonted thing!)
Holds out to us a helping, kindly hand,
Is lenient to our faults, and celebrates
Our first début in life, obsequiously
Receiving us and welcoming us as lord?
O fleeting days! like to a lightning flash
Extinguished swift.   What mortal man can be
Still unaware of woe, when once has fled
That fairest age, his sweetest time of life,
When youth, alas! his youth has passed away?

And doth not every spot, Nerina mine,
Whisper to me of thee?   Hast thou indeed
E'er faded from my thoughts?   Where art thou gone,
That all I find of thee, my darling, here
Is thy sweet memory?   Thy native place
Thee never more shall see, that window whence
Thou oft didst talk with me, and which reflects
The flickering, pale, sad glimmer of the stars
Is all deserted.   Where art thou that I
No longer hear thy voice as once I did,
When every accent faint that from thy lips
Soft fell, and reached mine ears, did summon up
Hot blushes on my cheeks?   These days are gone.
Thou art no more, my sweetest love!   Thou'st passed
Away!   To others now's allotted earth's
Sojourn, and others roam these sweet hillsides.
So swift thou'rt passed away, and like a dream _fleeting time_
Thy life has fled!   Thou tripp'dst along, thy face
Did beam with joy, and in thine eyes there shone
That dreamy, far-off, frank, true look, that light
Of youth, till Fate did quench them, and thou layst
All stark and cold!   Ah! in my heart still burns
The old love, Nerina mine.   If I at times
The festive dance and merry-making still
Frequent, I inward say, 'No more shalt thou,
Love, deck thee for the festive dance and throng.'
When May returns, and lovers offerings bring
Of nosegays and of song to their beloved,
I say, 'For thee, Nerina mine, shall spring
No more return for aye, and love no more!'

Each bright, glad day, each flowery wayside mead
I see, each joy I taste, but makes me say,
' Nerina doth rejoice no more ; for her
No more are fields and air.   Alas ! thou'rt gone
Eternal sigh of me, thou'rt gone ; for aye
Shall bitter memory be companion sole
To my each reverie sweet, my tender thrills,
My heart's each sad and dearly cherished throb !

NOCTURNAL ODE OF A WANDERING
SHEPHERD OF ASIA

O SILENT moon, what dost thou in the skies?
O moon, say what thou dost!
At eve thou dost arise
And scan the wastes, then to thy rest thou sinkst.
Art thou not sated yet
With thine eternal wandering that same way?
Is thy desire not weary with disgust
Of seeing these same vales?
So does the shepherd's life
Thy life resemble, moon.
He wakes at dawn of day,
His flock across the plain he leads, and sees
But flocks, and wells, and grass;
Then, tired, he lays him down when night is nigh,
Nor other hope he has.
O moon, tell me what boon
The shepherd's life brings him,
Or your life unto you? What purpose, pray,
Has my brief course or thy
Immortal, heavenly way?

The feeble old graybeard
In tatters and bare-foot,
Upon his shoulders bearing grievous load,
O'er mountain and through vale,
O'er hard, sharp rocks, deep sand and stubbly road,
By wind and storm, and scorching glare of sun,
And bitter, icy cold,
Doth, panting sore, swift run,
Through pools and torrents speeds,
And, stumbling, rises up, and hastes amain,
Without respite or hold,
All mangled and blood-stained, until he gain
The goal of all his toil
And moil, and weary way : the dread abyss
And vast, wherein he may
Plunge headlong, and annihilation find.
O virgin moon, but this
Is sad life's little day !

For trouble is man born,
And birth itself is nought but risk of death.
Life's first experience is
Of woe and pain, and from our earliest breath
It is our parents' heed
To compensate us for the ill fate of birth.
Then, as we grow in years,
They both sustain us, and in every way
They aim by word and deed
To cheer us for life's fray,
And reconcile us to this vale of tears.

No care more loving e'er
Do parents show their offspring on this earth.
But why bring to the light
Of day, why load with birth
Him who for life must after be consoled ?
If life's an evil thing,
Why should we to it cling ?
O most chaste moon, such is
Our mortal life's sad day !
But thou immortal art,
And maybe heedst but little what I say.

Yet thou, eternal wanderer and lone,
So pensive sad, mayhap dost comprehend
Our poor terrestrial fate,
Our sufferings, and all our sighs and moan.
Thou knowst what death is, last and pallid state
Of perishable things,
And passing from this earth, and last farewell
To each belovèd, old, familiar friend.
Thou doubtless, too, canst tell
The real why of things, and seest the fruit
Of morning and of eve,
The silent and infinite march of time.
Thou knowst, indeed, who from the sweetest spring
Doth bounteous gifts receive,
Whom summer's heat doth help, for whom her rime
And ice doth winter bring.
A thousand things thou knowst, and layest bare,
Which from the simple shepherd are hid deep.

Oft when I see thee there
Above the desert plains mute stand and gaze,
Which meet on every side the sky's expanse,
Or tend me with my sheep,
As slowly we from point to point advance,
And when I see the stars in heaven blaze,
I say within myself,
' Why all these torches' light ?
Why all the boundless air, and infinite
Blue firmament of heaven ?   What means that sky
Immense and desolate, and what am I ?'
Thus reason I within me of the vast
And boundless realms of space,
And of the innumerable starry host ;
Of so much restless moving and of toil
Of everything in heaven and on earth,
Wheeling without reprieve,
And aye returning to their former place.
No fruit can I perceive,
No use or purpose in it all.   But thou,
Immortal youth, thou knowest all, I trow,
And this *I* know and feel,
Whatever joy or weal
Another reaps from play
Of circling sphere, or my
Existence poor, to me life's sad alway.

O thou my blessed flock that tak'st thy rest,
And hast, methinks, no cares within thy breast,
How I do envy thee !

Not only in that thou
From sorrow sore seemst free,
And every pain and harm
Dost soon forget, and each most dread alarm,
But more that discontent thee never nears.
When thou liest in the shade upon the grass
Thou art so still and calm,
And in this state thy years
Without vexation thou dost mostly pass.
When in the shade upon the grass I sit
A weariness doth flit
Across my soul; I'm tortured as with rack
Or goad, so that I, sitting, farthest am
From finding peace or rest.
And yet, there's nought I lack
Or crave, nor hitherto have cause for plaint.
I cannot tell what joy,
Nor yet how great, is thine, but thou *art* blest.
I, too, have joy, though faint
It be, my flock—not that's my sole annoy.
If thou couldst speak, I'd ask of thee, ' O say,
Why doth it satisfy
Each animal to lie
At slothful ease, whilst I,
Outstretched at rest, to tediousness am prey ?'

Perchance had I the wings
Above the clouds to mount,
And one by one the stars in order count,
Or, lightning-like, from peak to peak to leap,

I should be happier, my belovèd sheep—
I should be happier, moon most white and fair.
Perchance my thought, the fate
Of others wondering, from the truth doth stray ;
Mayhap in any way,
In every state, in cradle or in lair,
To all that breathe cursed is their natal day !

REST AFTER STORM

THE storm is past and gone :
I hear birds' merry notes, and cackle gay
Of hens to the highway
Once more returned.   And there too a blue rift
Bursts through, above the mountain, in the west ;
The lowering vapours lift,
And in the valley bright the river gleams.
On every side with joy exults each breast :
The noises re-begin,
The wonted toil's renewed.
The workman, in his hands his tools, seems glued
To's door, the while he sings,
And scans the threat'ning sky ;
The women issuing forth to draw the rain
Fresh fallen zealous vie ;
The plant vendor now brings
His wares from lane to lane
Anew, with wonted cry.
The sun comes out again, and sparkles o'er
The hills and roofs.   The balconies once more

Re-ope, and terraces and galleries.
Along the road advancing, far away
I hear the sound of bells, the noise of wheels,
As back the trav'ller speeds his homeward way.

　Each heart is blithe and gay.
When else do we life feel
So sweet and full of joy?
Or to our books address
Ourselves with so much zeal,
Or bend to toil, or turn to new employ?
Or when do we our ills remember less?
Thou joy akin to pain,
Thou empty pleasure vain,
The fruit of past affright, whereby he who
Abhorred his life did quail
And 'fore death frighted quake;
And men sore tortured, pale
And numb, and mute did shake
With beating heart and beaded brow, when they
Beheld against them hurled
Heaven's bolts, wind, rain, and hail!

　So, courteous Nature, then
These are thy gifts, these are
The pleasures thou on men
So lavish shedst!   But fruit of pain's annoy
Is then our every joy!
Annoys thou scatterest with bounteous hand,
And pain spontaneous springs, and great that grand

Rich boon of pleasure which from woe is born,
By way of mighty miracle, at times !
O race of man to Heaven dear, 'tis weal
Enough if it but deign
Thee some respite from pain ;
Thou'rt blest if death thy every sorrow heal !

SATURDAY EVENING IN THE VILLAGE

BACK from the fields the young girl wends her way
At sunset, shouldering
Her sheaf of grass, whilst in her hand is borne
A lovely rose and gillyflower bouquet,
With which to-morrow morn
(For 'tis Sunday) she'll deck
And busk, as is her wont, her hair and neck.
The aged gossip sits
Upon the staircase with her friends and spins
In the ebbing light of day that slowly flits ;
And garrulous of her youthful days she prates,
When she, too, decked herself out for the fêtes,
And yet all hale and lithe
Was wont to trip it all the livelong eve
With sweethearts of those days so fair and blithe.
The air grows dim with night,
The clear sky darkens o'er, the shadows fall
Athwart, from house and hill,
Flung by the rising moon's pale, growing light.
Hark ! vesper bell rings in

The approaching festival ;
And at that sound the heart
With gladness seems to thrill.
Upon the square the crowd
Of urchins shouts aloud,
Making a merry din,
The while they skip and run ;
The workman, whistling soft a lively air,
Thinks of his day of rest,
The while he hies him to his frugal fare.

Then when each other light is quenched around,
And other sounds are stilled,
Hark to the thud of hammer, and the sound
Of joiner's saw, who plies
His work by dim lamplight at's bench, and hies
And hastes with all his might
His task to finish ere the dawn shall light.

Of all the seven this is the day most fraught
With gladd'ning hope and joy :
To-morrow will annoy
And sadness bring once more, when each one's thought
Will to the weary round of toil recur.

O playful little boy,
This golden youthful age
Of thine is like a day replete with joy,
A day serene and bright,
Precursor of thy life's gay, festive day !

Rejoice thy fill, my lad ; now's thy most sweet,
Most fair and happy stage.
This only do I wish : propitious may
Life's festival, tho' late it come, thee greet !

XXIV (26)

MY SOVEREIGN THOUGHT

Most sweet and potent lord,
Thou swayer of my mind's profoundest sphere ;
Most dread, but yet most dear
God's gift ; thou consort true
Of my lugubrious days,
O Thought, that art so oft before my gaze !

Who does not speak of thy
Mysterious nature ?   Who us men among
But feels thy might ?   Man's tongue
By what he feels is spurred
To tell what feelings e'er in him are stirred,
Yet each time deems he all's till now unheard.

How desolate and lone
My mind has been since thou
Didst choose thy residence therein to make !
Me all my other thoughts on every side
Did speedily forsake,
Quick as a lightning flash.   Like to a tower

Mid solitary plain
Thou standst alone, gigantic in thy power.

How petty, as compared with thee alone,
All man's works here below
And life itself too in my eyes have grown :
The unsufferable annoy
Of daily intercourse,
Of empty pleasure's empty hope, of time
Of ease, beside that joy
Which I derive from thee—that joy sublime !

As from the rocks all bare
Of rugged Apennine
The weary wand'rer turns his longing eye
On fields which smile afar, so green and fair ;
So I from coarse and dry
Communion with the world, with ready will,
As in a gladsome garden, to thee turn,
My senses to restore with thy sojourn.
Incredible it seems
To me that this sad life and senseless world
I could apart from thee
For so long time have borne ;
I cannot realize
An aspiration else
Than what resembles thee, or other sighs.

And now since first I learned
What this life means, by sad experience sore,
Dark death for me no terrors hath in store.

To-day but sport appears
To me that which this world
Of fools now praises, now abhors, and fears,
Life's last predestined bourne.
Let danger come, I'm ready to confront
Her every threat with smile of unconcern !

   I ever did revile
The coward, ignoble, vile
And abject soul.   At once now each act base
Doth prick me to the quick ;
My soul from every phase
Of man's depravity turns in disdain.
I feel myself above
This puffed up age that feeds on hopes so vain,
Is lover of buffoons, to virtue foe ;
Which for the useful yearns
Fool-like, and does not see
That life thereby more useless aye doth grow.
My mind the judgments spurns
Of men ; the fickle rabble I revile
And scorn—thy worshipful
Disparager, to all high thoughts hostile !

   What passion doth not yield
When thou dost take the field ?
What other passion's bliss
'Mong mortal men reigns comparable to this ?
Yea, greed and pride and hatred and disdain,
The lust of honour and of rule,

What but weak wishes vain
Are they compared with thee ?   One only fire
Enkindles us : with this,
Thou lord of most dread power,
The eternal laws the human heart did dower !

This life no value has, no aim except
Through thee, who man with every boon dost bless ;
Thou Fate dost justify
Alone, who placed us here
To suffer so much pain without redress ;
Through thee alone at times
Not stupid, brutal minds, but hearts refined
May feel that life can be than death more kind.

To taste thy joys ineffable, sweet Thought,
To fathom human pain,
And for long years sustain
This mortal life thou heldst me not unworth ;
And I would still hie back,
All sorely versed in human ills, given such
A beacon light, and re-begin life's track :
For, mid the sands and deadly bite of snake
Which swarm life's wilderness,
I never yet did take
Myself to thee, all tired, but such a weal
Aye seemed these woes and pains of ours to heal.

What world, what paradise,
What new infinity is this to which
Thy wondrous magic charm doth bid me rise

So oft ! in which I roam
Neath other than the known familiar light,
And sink earth's lot and home
And all the real in oblivion's night !
Such dreams as these, I seem
To think, have gods.   And, oh ! in fine a dream
In essence, lending beauty to stern truth,
Art thou, O most sweet Thought—
A wayward fancy's dream !   But yet in sooth,
Mid wingèd fancies sweet,
Thou art divine ; because so free and bold
Thou often with the real wrestlest hard,
And seemst as real as it,
Nor vanishest, till in death's lap enfold.

And thou wilt be, my Thought, thou vital spark
Alone unto my life,
Thou source beloved of sufferings infinite,
With me thro' death into the long night's dark ;
For in my soul I hear a deathless chord
Proclaim thou'rt given to be my endless lord.
Other delusions sweet
Aye more the real sight
Of things was wont to dull.   The more I see
Her, and returning greet
Her whom I live on, communing with thee,
The more that great delight,
That fevered passion grows, which is my breath.
Angelic beauty thou !
Each fairest face on which I gaze but seems

To imitate thy face,
Like to a picture poor.   Thou only spring
Of every other grace,
Methinks thou art earth's only beauteous thing!

Since I beheld thee first,
Hast thou not been the object aye supreme
Of my most serious care?   Did ever fly
An hour but that I thought of thee?   Have I
E'en to my dreams e'er let
Thy sovereign image lack?   Fair as a dream,
Shape from angelic sphere!
In tabernacle here,
In the glorious realms of the universe entire,
What hope I, or desire
More lovely than thine eyes to ever see?
To ever have more sweet than thought of thee?

XXV (27)

LOVE AND DEATH

'Ον οἱ θεοι φιλοῦσιν ἀποθνῄσκει νέος
'Whom the gods love dies young'

Twin brothers, Love and Death, both at one birth
Did Fate bear to the Earth.
The world no other thing
So fair holds here below, nor yet the stars.
Blessings from one doth spring,
And the supremest joys
That in the realms of being e'er were seen ;
The other each sore pain,
Each grievous ill destroys.
That maid of fairest form,
Most sweet to look upon,
Not such as craven man her represents,
Oft Love, that youthful swain,
Doth walk with, by his side,
And o'er life's journey they together glide,
Chief comforts of each wise, right-hearted man.
We men are ne'er more wise

Than when we're smit by love, nor stronger than
When life's woes we despise ;
Nor for another lord
Are we prepared so many risks to run ;
For where thou dost afford
Thy aid, Love, courage springs,
Or reawakes ; not wise in idle thoughts,
As is their wont, but wise in actions then
Becomes the race of men.

When first his fierce, fell fire
And flame Love doth impart
Unto the deep-moved heart,
Along with him a languid, tired desire
For Death doth come, and sore the breast oppress.
I know not how, but such
The first effect of true love's potent touch.
Perchance life's wilderness
Doth then appal the eye.   This earth perchance
Man as impossible for aye askance
Doth eye, without that new,
Strange bliss his fancies form—
That joy unique he hopes shall never cease.
But yet on her account a violent storm
Foreboding in his heart, he yearns for peace,
For refuge from the doom
That coming storm doth brew,
E'en roaring now, and shrouding all in gloom.

Then when all round is cloaked
By its dread, awful might,

And cares invincible the heart assail,
How oft art thou invoked,
O Death, how oft desired
With passionate yearning by sad lover's wail!
At dawn how oft, at night
How oft, surrendering his body tired,
He'd happy deem himself if from his bed
He ne'er should lift his head
Again, and no more see day's bitter light!
And often at the toll of funeral bell
Or dirge chant, which the dead
Escorts unto the grave's eternal sleep,
He, heaving sighs more deep
From his heart's core, doth envy him who goes
Away amongst departed shades to dwell.
Even the senseless mob,
The rustic boor, who knows
Naught of the virtues which from wisdom spring,
And e'en the maid, so timid late and coy,
Who at Death's very name
Felt stand on end her hair,
Now dares upon the tomb and funeral bands
To fix her eye with firm and steady gaze;
On steel and poison doth dare
To meditate at length,
And in her untrained mind
The gentleness of Death she understands.
So much are men inclined
By discipline of Love to Death! And oft
The heart's love-fever reaches such a height

It can no more be borne by mortal strength;
Then yields man's body frail
To its dread thrills, and by the potent might
Of his fierce brother thus doth Death prevail;
Or Love so strikes their bosoms' deepest chord,
That rustic ignorant and tender maid
Of their own fixed, accord
Lay violent hands upon
Their lives, and reach the longed for early tomb.
At their fate laughs the world,
On which be Heaven's peace, old age its doom!

All earnest, happy, bold,
And true men, noble-souled,
May Fate with one or other of you dower,
Ye most sweet lords and friends
Of the sad race of man,
To whose no other power may be compared,
Whose might none else in the wide universe
Excels but that of Fate!   And thou my tongue
Has ever honoured, since my years began,
And ever has invoked,
Fair Death, that here below
Alone on earth dost pity mortal woe,
If I have ever sung
Thy praise; if I thy majesty divine,
Shamed by the ungrateful crowd,
Have tried to vindicate,
Delay no more; incline
To such unwonted prayers;

Close these sad eyes of mine
From light, O Queen of endless days !
Whate'er the hour thou hearst my prayer, thou'lt
    find
Me ready in thy wings to be enfold—
With head erect, 'gainst Fate
Armed with defiance bold,
The hand not licking which doth wield the whip,
And in my blood doth dip,
Nor heaping it with praise
And thanks, as are the ways
Of men inured to cringing from of old ;
But every empty hope far from me hurled,
Wherewith this childish world
Consoles itself, I'll thee alone attend,
Till ends this night of pain ;
And calm await the day
When I shall wrap me, lulled to endless rest,
In thy pure virgin breast !

XXVI (28)

TO MY HEART

Now rest thee evermore,
My weary heart! My last delusion's dead,
Which I eternal deemed. 'Tis perishèd.
My each fond hugged deceit
Has lost all charm, and e'en desire is dead.
Rest thee for aye! Thou'st beat
And throbbed enough. There's not one thing that's
    worth
A thrill from thee, and not one sigh this earth
Deserves. Life's but annoy
And bitterness; this world's vain joys soon cloy.
Rest thee for aye! Despair
With thy last beat! Fate has bequeathed the tomb
As her one boon to man. That hated force
Occult, which all doth doom
To woe; and vanity, that sure-set bourne
Reserved for all, thee, Nature, ever scorn.

XXVII (29)

ASPASIA

Aspasia mine, thy image oft returns
Before mine eyes !   Mayhap amid the crowd
It flashes fleeting on me in the face
Of others ; or amid the lonely fields
In clear daylight, or 'neath the silent stars,
As if by sweetest harmony evoked,
That lofty vision bursts upon my soul,
Nigh blinded with the o'erpowering, dazzling sight.
How fondly adored, ye gods ; how much one day
My passion and delight !   I never feel
Sweet perfume from beflow'red banks arise,
Or fragrant smelling air in city streets,
But I behold thee as thou wert that day
When, welcomed in the gaily furnished rooms,
All redolent of fresh spring flowers, thou, clad
In dusky, violet-coloured gown, didst burst
Upon my gaze in angel guise, outstretched
On soft, sleek furs, voluptuous and sweet
Mysterious thrills exhaling from thy form ;
And when thou, skilled enchantress, didst imprint

Warm sounding kisses on the puckered lips
Of thy sweet babes, thy snowy neck the while
Extending, and with thy most graceful hand
Didst hug them to thy bosom coyly hid
And waking sweet desires.   Then opened first
To my soul's ravished vision a new heaven,
New earth and a divine-like light.   Thus too
In my well shielded heart thy hand did drive
Amain the shaft, which, rooted deep, I bore
With bitter smart, until upon that day
Of woe the twice revolving sun had risen.

　　Thy beauty, lady, burst upon my sight
Like ray divine !   A like effect's produced
By beauty and by music's harmonies,
Which seem to oft reveal the mystery deep
Of hid Elysiums.   Then the sore-hit swain
Doth amorously upon the offspring sweet
Of's fancy, love's ideal, gaze, which doth
Embrace a foretaste of Heaven's paradise,
And likens all in face, and mien, and voice
To that sweet lady whom the ravished youth
Believes he loves with doting, vague desire.
And yet it is not she, but his ideal
That he enfolds in his embrace and loves.
At length of the false object of his love
And of his error ware, he fumes, and oft
The lady wrongly blames.   A woman's mind
To this ideal high doth rarely rise ;
Nor can a woman know or understand

What passion her own beauty doth inspire
In lover noble-souled.   Such thought can ne'er
Her narrow mental vision penetrate.
The swain beguiled does wrong to pin his faith
On that keen flashing of those soft, sweet eyes,
Or hope for hidden depths of sense, and more
Than man's, in her whom Nature has decreed
To man inferior every way.   If she
A gracefuller and tenderer form received,
She also has a weaker intellect.

   Nor, O Aspasia, canst thou have e'er yet
Imagined what a fire thou for a time
Enkindledst in my heart !   Thou canst not know
What boundless love, or what intense sweet pains,
What thrills ineffable, what rapturous joys
Thou stirr'dst in me ; nor shall the time e'er come
That thou shalt know !   So the musician, who
Sweet harmonies doth execute, knows not
The effect produced upon his auditor
By's hand and voice.   Now, that Aspasia's dead,
Whom I so fondly loved !   She's gone for aye,
Dear object of my life awhile ! and yet
From time to time, like phantom form beloved,
She's wont to come and vanish quick.   Thou liv'st,
Not only lovely still, but lovely so
That thou all others in my eyes excelst.
But yet that passion sprung from thee is dead :
For 'twas not *thee* I loved, but that Divine
Ideal once my heart gave life to, now

A tomb.　'Twas *she* I long adored, and her
Celestial beauty so entrancèd me,
That, though from the beginning well aware
Of thy nature, thine arts, and thy deceits,
Yet, gazing on her lovely eyes in thine,
I paid thee slavish court the while she lived ;
Not lured astray indeed, but, by delight
In that resemblance beautiful, beguiled
A long and bitter bondage to endure.

　　Now boast it, for thou mayst !　Tell how thou art
Thy sex's one ensample who prevailed
To bend my lofty head ; to whom my heart,
As yet unstormed, I offered free !　Aye, say
How thou sawst bend my suppliant eyes, the first
And last—so be it !—time ; how at thy feet,
All bashful, tremulous (I blush with shame
And scorn in telling it !), beside myself,
I like a faithful cur watched every wish
Of thine, each word and act ; grew pale at thy
Proud scorn's displeasure ; how I beamed with joy
At thy mere courteous nod ; and countenance
And colour changed at thy each glance !　The charm
Is broke, and shattered with it is my yoke,
And dashed aground !—whereat I joy.　And I,
At length my bondage overthrown, my long
Mad doting, now contentedly embrace
Wisdom and liberty, though full of pain.
For though our life, of sweet delusions reft
And love, is like a starless, winter's night,

It is to me sufficient comfort, yea,
Revenge enough on Fate, here on the grass
To lie, at ease and motionless, and gaze
And smile upon the earth, and sea, and sky.

XXVIII (30)

ON AN ANCIENT TOMBSTONE BAS-RELIEF

REPRESENTING A YOUNG LADY ON THE POINT OF
DEATH BIDDING HER FRIENDS FAREWELL

WHITHER art bound, sweet maid?
Who calls thee far away
From all thy kindred dear?
Alone, and so betimes wilt thou forsake
Thy father's house and go? wilt thou one day
Revisit these abodes, and render glad
Those who around thy bed now weep so sad?

   Thine eyes are tearless, undismayed thy mien,
Yet thou art sorrowful. Whether the way
Be bright or dismal, cheerful or full of gloom
The refuge of the tomb,
From thy sad looks we may
Glean nought thereof. Alas! nor can I prove,
Nor has the world perhaps determined yet
Whether thou hast incurred Heaven's hate or love,
Or whether it were best
To think of thee as blessèd or unblest.

Death calls thee ; at the threshold of life's morn
Is thy grave's gate and death.   Thou mayst not see
Thy home again, nor face
Of dear relation e'er
Behold for aye.   Thy place
Is with the buried dead :
For all time shall thy dank abode be there !
Mayhap thou'rt blest ; but who shall moralize
Upon thy fate, and grudge to thee his sighs !

Light never to behold
Were surely preferable.   But being born,
To die when beauty just began to unfold
In limb and countenance,
And from afar the world
Before her bow in lowly reverence ;
When every hope was budding, and before
Reality his dismal bolts had hurled
Upon her radiant head ; to disappear
As if she'd never been, like vapour formed
On the horizon into fleecy clouds
That quickly fade away ; and to exchange
Her future promise fair
For the thick darkness of the silent tomb ;
If such a fate seem blest,
Grasped by pure reason's range,
It fills with pity deep the hardest breast.

Nature, thou mother dread,
Who formst for tears thy creatures from their birth,

Thou marvel of our eulogies unworth,
Who bringest forth and rearest but to kill,
If death untimely be
An evil, why delightest thou to see
Die such sweet innocence?
If good, why is't so dread,
Why more than other ill
Do those who die such parting bitter find?
Why inconsolable those left behind?

The whole creation yearns
For rest from pain, accursed where'er it turns,
Where'er it refuge seeks !
Thy will was law to thee
That youthful hope should be
By life deluded, and life's course should run
Replete with cares ; that death should be the one
Defence 'gainst ills ; this the sure destined bourne,
The immutable decree
Thou setst to human life.   Alas ! why, when
The fevered race is o'er, not grant to men
At least a happy end ? instead, why dress
In dismal pall, and gird
With mournful gloom her that our hearts confess,
While yet in life's full bloom,
To be our future doom,
And that we mid life's woe
Our only solace know ?
Why should the port loom dread,
More than the raging billows' flood, ahead ?

Yet if death be an ill,
Which thou unto us all
Reservest after launching us, unasked,
Unskilled, on life, without our fault or will,
The dead have surely a more envious lot
Than those who're left to grieve
For their beloved.   For if indeed 'tis true,
As I most firm believe,
That death's a boon and good,
And life an evil thing, who ever could,
E'en though this duty's clear,
Desire the death of those he holds so dear,
Thus crippled to be left
And of his best part reft;
Or see across the threshold sadly borne
That sweet, belovèd form
With whom he spent so many happy years;
And say his last farewell, of hope forlorn
Of meeting her again
Upon life's troublous sea;
Then, left alone upon this vale of tears,
Gaze mutely round, and feel each well-known place,
Each hour recall his dead love's memory?
Ah, Nature, ah! how could thy heart endure
To wrench from fond embrace
A friend away from's friend,
A father from his child,
Brother from brother dear,
Lover from his beloved : and one being ta'en,
To leave the other lone?   How couldst thou lend

Thyself to inflict such pain
On us so needlessly, as that a man
Survive his friend?　But this is Nature's plan,
To judge her by her deeds,
That other than our weal or woe she heeds.

XXIX (31)

ON THE PORTRAIT OF A BEAUTIFUL LADY

CARVED ON HER TOMBSTONE

Such wert thou ! now beneath
Thou liest a skeleton and dust.   Above
Thy bones and mould, immovably set up
In vain, stands mute and wond'ring at the flight
Of years, the image of
Thy faded beauty, like the guardian sprite
Of grief and mem'ry only.   That sweet glance
Which, bent on men, as now it seems, made beat
Their hearts tumultuously ; that lip whereon,
As from an urn replete,
Bliss seems to overflow ; that neck, the throne
Already of desire ; that lovely hand,
At whose clasp oft has grown
Frigid another's hand with too much bliss ;
That bosom at whose sight
A pallor blanched the cheeks of smitten wight,
Once stirred with life : now mould
And bones art thou ; the sad
And hateful sight a stone doth now withhold.

To such pass doth Fate bring
That form which, whilst amongst us, seemed most
    like
To the divine.   Eternal mystery
Of being!   Beauty grows to-day, the spring
Ineffable of lofty, boundless thoughts
And sentiments, and seems,
Like radiance that outstreams
From some celestial presence on this earth,
To give mortality
The symbol and sure hope
Of golden worlds and blessed destiny,
Of superhuman fate :
To-morrow, by a breath,
That which like some angelic form so late
Appeared grows hideous, vile,
And hateful to behold,
And from the mind the while
Those wondrous thoughts depart
Which took therefrom their essence and their start.

   Mid roaming fancies' realms
Skilled harmony gives birth
To infinite desires
And lofty visions, by its native worth ;
And so the human soul mysteriously
Through floods of rapture floats,
Like to some swimmer bold
Who on the ocean's breast disports himself ;
But if discordant notes

Assail the ear, behold,
That paradise is shattered in a trice.

If thou'rt but dust, O man,
And empty shadow, vile
And wholly frail, how can
Such lofty intuitions e'er be thine?
But if thou'rt part divine,
How can each noble thought and high instinct
Of thine by cause so base
Be roused so lightly, and so soon extinct?

XXX (33)

THE SETTING OF THE MOON

As in the lonely night,
O'er fields and river bathed in silvern light,
Where zephyr breezes blow,
And countless vague landscapes
And weird and ghostly shapes
The distant shadows throw
Beneath the waters still
And boughs and hedges, house and hill—
Come to Tyrrhene's confines,
Or heaven's, behind the Alps or Apennines,
In the infinite womb
The moon doth sink ; and all the world grows
    pale ;
The shadows fly, and vale
And hill are shrouded in a deepest gloom ;
The night is left all lone ;
The waggoner doth greet with mournful song
The parting radiance of the fading gleam,
Which guides no more his team
Their solitary homeward way along ;

So youth too disappears
And quits man's mortal years.
His fond delusions grope
Their way in flight like shades
And phantom shapes ; no longer in him springs
The fount of far-off Hope,
To which our mortal nature fondly clings.
All desolate and drear
This life is left.   The wildered traveller,
As in its darkness he doth vainly peer,
Looks for some end or goal along the road
Which stretches far and lone·;
And feels this life's abode
To him, as he to it, is stranger grown.

Too happy and too bright
Would seem in Heaven's sight
Our miserable lot, if our youth's prime,
Where every boon from thousand pains doth spring,
Should last the full extent of our lifetime.
Too gentle that decree
Would be which dooms to death each breathing
    thing,
If half our little span
Were not given us to be
Than dreaded death a far more cruel ban.
The eternal gods old age
Invented, of all woes
The crown, idea for immortal brains
Most meet, in which the throes

Of sweet desire should be unknown, and dead
All hope, dried up the wells of joy, our pains
Aye greater grown, and comforts all be fled.

And you, ye hills and dales,
Of that effulgence of the west bereft,
Which silvered o'er night's veil,
Not long shall ye be left
Thus orphaned; soon from out the east ye'll hail
Returning light new pierce
The darksome heavens, and the dawn fresh break!
The morning sun close following in its wake,
And flashing round him fierce
His powerful, flaming darts,
Will bathe with floods of gold
Both you and the ethereal plains of heaven.
But this our mortal life, when once departs
Youth's fairest sun, may never more behold
Another light arise, or other dawn ;
'Tis widowed to the end.   To symbolize
The night which wraps in gloom
Dead centuries, the gods have placed the tomb!

XXXI (34)

THE GENISTA

OR, THE FLOWER OF THE DESERT

Καὶ ἠγάπησαν οἱ ἄνθρωποι μᾶλλον τὸ σκότος ἢ τὸ φῶς.

'And men loved darkness rather than light.'—ST. JOHN iii. 19.

HERE on the barren ridge
Of Mount Vesuvius dread,
Exterminator fell,
Whereon nor tree nor other flower may bloom,
Thou all around thy lonesome shrubs dost spread,
O sweetly smelling broom,
Despising not the waste !   So I beheld
Thy stems adorn the country desolate
Which girds around that state
That in her sovereign sway the earth once held ;
And thou seemst to inspire
The trav'ller, by thy sad and solemn look,
With memory's visions of that lost empire.
Again I see thee in this spot, the friend
Of lonely places by the world forsook—

Afflicted fortune's comrade to the end !
These plains with dust
Of barren ash bestrewed, and overspread
With stony lava crust,
Which echo underneath the wand'rer's tread,
Where snakes do weave their coils and bask i' the sun,
And where, among the rocks,
The rabbits to their well-known burrows run,
Were tilled fields and gay streets—
Here waved the yellowing grain ; here lowing kine
Once roamed, and bleating flocks ;
Here palaces and gardens fine,
Whose pleasant, cool retreats
Tired princes sought, here famous cities stood,
Which the avenging mountain buried deep,
Out-belching from her jaws her fiery flood,
With all their denizens.   So all around
Is laid in ruined heap,
Where thou, sweet flower, a settlement hast found,
And, as if pitying others' loss, a smell
Of sweetest perfume thou to heaven dost raise,
And cheerst the desert waste.   To this bleak ridge
Let him repair whose wont it is with praise
To vaunt our human lot ; then let him tell
How much 'tis Nature's heed
Our helpless race to spare !   The feeble sway,
Too, wielded by man's seed
He may in measure adequate here weigh,
Which, when it least doth dread, the Mother stern
Doth in a moment with a nod o'erturn,

And can, with effort not
Much greater, in the twinkling of an eye
Entire annihilate.
Here writ on every spot
Of earth you may descry
Man's each '*magnificent, progressive fate.*'

'Proud, senseless age, come look
Upon thine image here,
Which hast the path forsook
Till now by thought's renascence marked out clear,
And turning thy footsteps the way they came,
Didst boast thy face about,
And progress didst it name !
The wits come fawning on thee all, their sire
By virtue of their dire
Sad fate, the while they flout
Such twaddle in their hearts.
With shame like this I'll not sink in the grave,
Tho' I might ape with ease
Their words, and vieing with their cringing rave,
And prate in phrases smooth thine ear to please :
Far rather that disdain which doth reside
Within my breast of thee,
As far as in me lies, I'll open show ;
Although full well I know
Oblivion is his lot who sore doth chide
His age.   Alike to me
And thee that evil is, which I despise.
Thou dreamst of Liberty, and yet wouldst Thought

Enfetter once again,
By which alone we rise
From servile bonds, and culture amongst men
Alone grows more ; which doth the common lot
Alone ameliorate.
The truth did bitter smack
As to the grievous fate and humble state
Which Nature gave us.   Thus it was thy back
Thou, like a dastard, turnedst to the light
Which did that truth proclaim, and in thy flight
Giv'st him the name of vile
Who follows it, and them
Alone callst great of soul,
Who, flouting others or themselves, through wile
Or folly, to the stars man's lot extol.

The man of poor estate and feeble frame,
But of a noble soul and lofty mind,
Doth neither deem nor name
Himself a man of wealth
Or strength, nor makes a laughable display
Of splendour, or of health
Amongst his fellow-kind ;
He's not ashamed to show and call himself,
In converse with the world, of power and pelf
A beggar, and in light of day his all
Rates at its real worth.
Not noble him I call,
But fool, who, from the birth
To perish doomed, and reared in sorrow, says :

Lo ! born for bliss I am !
And doth the journals cram
With filthy pride, and promises on earth
Exalted destinies, in heaven unknown,
Far less on earth, and joys
Undreamt, to men whom plash
Of stormy sea, one breath
Of poisoned air, or subterranean crash
So utterly destroys,
That scarce their memory survives their death.
Of noble soul is he
Who doth our common fate
With dauntless aspect dare
Confront, and who with utterance full and free,
That all the truth shall state,
The ill confesses given to us in share,
And our low, frail estate ;
Who bold and strong and brave
His suffering bears, nor by his brother's hate
And wrath—an ill more grave
Than any—doth enlarge
His own misfortunes, in that he doth blame
His fellows for his woes, but lays the charge
On the true culprit, whom we mother name
Of men by birth, stepmother in good will.
Her he calls enemy ; and knowing well
Society allied
Against assaults from her, and up in arms,
He deems his fellows tied
In one confederacy against all harms,

And lovingly enfolds
Them in his arms, and holds
A strong and ready hand to them ; no less
He in the shifting chance and change and stress
Of the common war expects ; and for the fray
'Gainst brothers his right hand to arm, and snares
And traps for them to lay
He deems as foolish as, on field beset
With hostile army, someone should forget
The foe at hottest stage
Of the onset, and against his friends should dare
Encounters fierce to wage,
And fellow-soldiers with fell slaughter smite
And turn in headlong flight.
When thoughts like these as clear
Become as once to the great bulk of men,
And that primeval fear
Which 'gainst fell Nature drew
Men close at first in social bonds, again
In part, by wisdom true,
Shall be led back, then shall the loyal, good,
True human brotherhood,
And justice and religion other root
Acquire once more than proud and vain conceits,
Foundation where is wont to plant its foot
The righteousness of man,
And stand as best what rests on error can.

Oft on these lonely slopes,
In mourning vesture clad

By the stark sea, which seems to undulate,
I sit by night, and o'er the sombre down
Out on the stars I gaze
That in the clear, blue firmament bright blaze,
Which far the mirroring sea
Reflects; and see a whole world scintillate
Around of sparks, resplendent space's crown.
Then when my eyes on these bright spheres I cast,
Which seem to them a dot,
But are so grandly vast
That earth and sea beside them are but spots
In truth, to which man not
Alone, but this whole globe,
On which man counts for nought,
Are totally unknown; and when I note
Those still more, nay infinitely, remote
Grouped constellation knots
Which seem to us but mist, to which not man
And not this earth alone, but all our stars,
In magnitude and number infinite,
Together with the gold orb of the sun,
Are all unknown, or else appear but as
A speck of nebulous light,
As these seem to our earth, then to my thoughts ·
How small seemst thou, O son
Of man! When I recall
Thy lot too here below, of which the dust
I tread is emblem; on the other hand
That thou thyself dost trust
To be the destined lord and goal of All;

How oft thy pride with fables too thou'st puffed
Of how down to this abject grain of sand
Called earth, the Authors of the universe
Came for thy sake, and affable converse
Oft held with men ; and how thou hast rebuffed
The wise with insults, thy derisive dreams
Renewing, till this present age which seems
All others to excel
In culture and wisdom ; I cannot tell
What impulse to thee then, unhappy race of men,
What feeling this my heart in fine assails—
If laughter 'tis or pity that prevails !

    As tiny apple falling from its stem,
In mellow autumntide,
Whose very ripeness urges it aground,
Unaided else, doth crush and void, and hide
Of an ant tribe the sweet
Abode, dug out with toil
Laborious in the soft and yielding soil ;
The works and riches, too, this busy corps
Had emulous striven in summertime to store
Destroying in a trice ;
So ashes, lava, stones menacing doom
And night, with boiling hot
Showers intermixed, and shot
Straight up to heaven from the rumbling womb,
And falling sheerly down ;
Or o'er the mountain side,
Fierce surging through the grass

A mighty overflow
Of liquid molten mass,
Of fusèd metals, and of red-hot sand
Did in a flash o'erthrow
And bury deep the cities which the sea
Once washed, there where the land
Slopes gently to the shore.
The grass now on their very sites is grazed
By goats, and other towns
Rise from the further shore, to which the razed
And buried walls are footstools, which the mount
Proud tramples underfoot, as 'twere, and frowns.
Nature man's seed doth count
Of no more worth or heed
Than ants : and if 'gainst him than them more rare
Her havoc fell doth fare,
The only reason is
Of this that far less num'rous is man's breed.

Since these haunts disappeared
Of teeming men, by the igneous flood o'erwhelmed,
Have passed away full eighteen hundred years ;
The peasant all alert
For's vineyards' sake, which mid these fields scarce
    rears
A soil with cinders sown and all inert,
Suspicious looks doth stretch
Up towards the fatal peak,
Which still stands awesome there, not yet grown
    meek,

Whose threatening cone destruction still doth bode
To him and his, and hearth and home so bare.
And often the poor wretch
Doth spend a sleepless night
Out in the open air,
His bed the roof of his poor, mean abode ;
And starting up full oft, the course explores
Of that eruption dread, which seething pours
From the abysmal womb
Upon the sandy ridge, which far away
Doth mirror Capri's shore
And Mergellina and fair Naples' Bay.
And if he see it near, or in the floor
Of his domestic well he hear the roar
Of bubbling, boiling water, he doth wake
His wife and sons in haste, and quick doth take
Whatever he can snatch at hand, and flees ;
His dear-loved home he sees
Afar, and nestling farm,
Which was his only source of livelihood,
A prey to the red flood
Which roaring ever nears, and pitiless
O'er them inexorably for aye doth spread !
After her long long sleep
Entombed Pompeii, dead
Like skeleton sunk deep,
Which piety or greed
Of land bares to the day,
Again basks in Heaven's light and sunbeam's ray ;
And from the Forum lone

Directly at the base
Of rows of lopped-off colonnades,
The stranger long upon the twofold cone
And smoking crest doth gaze,
Which to the sprawling ruins still threats doom.
And in the horror of the dark night's gloom
Through empty theatres,
And temples mutilate and broken porch
And hall, wherein the bat conceals her young,
Like weird, ill-omened torch
Which boding thro' bare palaces is swung,
The direful lava stream doth rush and flare,
Whose far-off ruddy glare
Pierces the gloom, and all around doth light.
Thus knowing nought of man, or of the flight
Of ages he calls old, or how grandsons
In time succeed grandsire,
Nature stands ever green, or rather runs
Down such a lengthy road
She seems to stand.   And meanwhile realms expire,
And tongues and nations fade : she nothing heeds :
And on eternity's vain boast man feeds !

  And thou, Genista lithe,
Which with thy fragrant groves
This bare and dreary country dost bedeck,
Soon thou beneath the cruel blow thy neck,
Laid low by subterranean fire, wilt droop,
When it the well-known road
Once more rewends, and greedy pall will spread

O'er thy soft, yielding woods.   And thou wilt stoop
Thy powerless, innocent, resistless head
Beneath its fatal load :
But yet at least wilt not have cringed in vain
Till then, like to a craven suppliant,
Before the future conqueror ; nor strain
Thy gaze with impious pride towards the stars,
Nor cower upon the waste,
Where Fortune, not thy will,
Brought thee to birth, and thy abode has placed ;
But wiser thou, and far
Less weak than man, in that thou didst not prate
That thy shoots delicate
By Fate, or of thyself, immortal are !

THE END.

BILLING AND SONS, LTD., PRINTERS, GUILDFORD.

Lightning Source UK Ltd.
Milton Keynes UK
UKHW022015111019
351469UK00007B/38/P